FIRST DEGREE

From Med School to Murder:
The Story Behind the Shocking
Will Sandeson Trial

KAYLA HOUNSELL

NIMBUS
PUBLISHING
— NIMBUS.CA —

Nimbus Publishing Limited
PO Box 9166
Halifax, NS, B3K 5M8
(902) 455-4286
nimbus.ca

Editor: Elaine McCluskey; Proofreader: Paula Sarson
Cover photo: Andrew Vaughan
Cover design: Heather Bryan
Interior design: John van der Woude, JVDW Designs
NB1345

Library and Archives Canada Cataloguing in Publication

Hounsell, Kayla, 1985-, author
First degree : from medical school to murder : the story
behind the shocking Will Sandeson trial / Kayla Hounsell.

Issued in print and electronic formats.
ISBN 978-1-77108-666-0 (softcover).—ISBN 978-1-77108-667-7 (HTML)

1. Sandeson, Will. 2. Samson, Taylor. 3. Murder—Nova Scotia—Halifax. 4. Trials (Murder)—Nova Scotia—Halifax. I. Title.

HV6535.C33H34 2018   364.152′309716225   C2018-902897-1
                                           C2018-902898-X

Nimbus Publishing acknowledges the financial support for its publishing activities from the Government of Canada, the Canada Council for the Arts, and from the Province of Nova Scotia. We are pleased to work in partnership with the Province of Nova Scotia to develop and promote our creative industries for the benefit of all Nova Scotians.

Dedicated in memory of Taylor Samson.

May we not forget that wrapped up in the pages of this crime thriller, a mother and father lost a son, a brother lost his protector, and a young man lost his life.

AUTHOR'S NOTE

This book is not a transcript of the trial, nor does it propose to cover every detail of the trial. When lawyers present evidence in court, the order sometimes depends on the availability of witnesses. As such, the order of some of the testimony has been changed to provide clarity to the story. The facts and context of the testimony have not been altered.

CONTENTS

CHAPTER 1
INTERROGATION

One of first things investigators learn about William Sandeson is that he is interested in medicine. Corporal Jody Allison is in Ontario on another matter when he receives a call asking him to interview the twenty-two-year-old. Allison lands at the Halifax airport and drives straight to police headquarters on Gottingen Street. It is around 11:30 P.M. on August 18, 2015. Another officer is interviewing Sandeson in relation to a missing persons case. Allison has a brief meeting with the lead investigators and then goes home to catch a few hours of sleep before returning to the station at 6 A.M. Allison knows Sandeson has been accepted to Dalhousie University's medical school and is about to start classes any day. He also knows Sandeson spent some time at a med school in the Caribbean. He decides to use this information as a strategy.

William Sandeson, who often goes by Will, is already waiting for Corporal Allison in an interview room, but he has no idea what is about to occur. The five-foot-ten, one-hundred-and-fifty-pound, blond-haired, blue-eyed varsity athlete works at a group home for adults who live with disabilities. He has no criminal record.

GOOD COP

Allison, clean-shaven with salt-and-pepper short coiffed hair, enters the eight-by-eight interrogation room in plain clothes: pants and a collared shirt with a sport jacket, no tie. He's not a big guy. The room contains two chairs with cameras mounted on the walls.

"How's it going there, Will?" He introduces himself as an officer with the RCMP in Halifax and tells Sandeson he's looking a little bit scared or nervous.

He asks Sandeson if he knows why he's been arrested. Sandeson, wearing sneakers, beige pants, and a blue-green T-shirt, says that he does. At this point, he's being questioned for kidnapping, trafficking, and misleading police.

"You were in your first year of being a medical doctor, right? So I take it that you're somewhat educated," Allison begins.

Sandeson says he's completed five years of post-secondary.

"So you're aware of all the different technology out there I'm sure, being a first-year medical student."

The officer asks Sandeson if he's ever watched csi. Perhaps, in another sign of technological advancements, Sandeson says he doesn't have a TV.

But Allison won't back down on the point.

"Okay, but you would be familiar, I mean. csi, a lot of what you see on that program is true; it's just that some of the stuff takes a little longer, you know, they get it done in a half an hour in the show, where it takes, in real life, a lot longer than that."

Allison is explaining to Sandeson that officers have already entered his apartment. He describes how police use DNA samples and fingerprints.

"There's nobody else that has the same fingerprint as me," he says. "Nobody else." He tells Sandeson that fingerprints used to be the "gold standard," that no matter what you do to your finger, your fingerprint will grow back the same. "But you know all this," he tells the promising young man seated before him.

Then Allison moves on to DNA, explaining that one of the first times it was used in Canada was in the case of Allan Legere, a New Brunswick serial killer. Legere killed five people between 1986 and 1989, when he was finally arrested. Due to the brutality of his crimes, he was called the Monster of the Miramichi.

"I know the guy," Allison tells Sandeson, explaining that DNA was used to convict Legere. "There's always something that the suspect leaves behind," he goes on, "and there's always something that the suspect takes with them."

Sandeson just sort of nods in agreement.

Allison also tells Sandeson that experts can do calculations to figure out what happened, based on how much blood there is and where it landed. Sandeson seems to be following along, chiming in that he knows they can determine things based on the velocity of the spatter. Allison continues that even if people try to clean up, blood may still be there years later.

It seems to be a warning of some kind, but the officer also seems to be trying to bond with Sandeson, telling him he has an aunt who has special needs and that he knows it takes a special kind of person to work with people who have special needs, as Sandeson does.

"I give props to anybody that can go in there and have the patience, and basically a good heart. I think you've got a good heart," Allison tells Sandeson. "I think that sometimes people, for whatever reason, they make some mistakes."

By all accounts, William Sandeson comes from a good family. His parents own a farm in Truro, his mother works for the Nova Scotia government in the Department of Agriculture and was the president of the local Rotary Club. He is the eldest of four boys. Unlike Allan Legere, he has never been in trouble with the law.

"There's times for whatever reason that things don't go quite as planned," Allison continues. "Actually if you think about it, things never go quite as planned, right, Will? They never go quite as planned."

Then it comes back to the medicine. It always comes back to the medicine.

Allison asks Sandeson what specifically his aspirations are, whether he wants to be a GP, a surgeon, etc. Sandeson responds with two words only, "sports medicine."

Allison acknowledges that that will take a long time, nearly a decade of Sandeson's life, while his buddies are all out making money. "So why does anyone want to become a doctor?" Allison asks. "You know why? Because they genuinely want to help people."

That's when he produces the Hippocratic Oath, a pledge taken by doctors in which they swear to uphold certain ethical standards. "You must have read it before, right?"

Sandeson says he knows the synopsis.

"The thing about it is that this whole thing is based around helping other people," the officer tells Sandeson, going on to draw out certain points from the lengthy script. "When you're looking after the patient, you don't do them any harm."

Then for the first time, Allison mentions the man who is missing—six-foot-five, two-hundred-and-twenty-pound Taylor Samson.

"Do you know Taylor's brother?"

"I didn't really know Taylor."

"Taylor's brother has an intellectual disability. He's missing his brother and he's a mess. Somebody's got to explain to him what happened, what happened to Taylor."

Sandeson stares in silence.

Allison continues, telling Sandeson he knows things aren't always as they appear. He uses an analogy, trying to compare a doctor's work to that of a police officer's.

"It's sort of like when somebody comes into the emergency room and presents with a chest pain. You're the attending physician, and you're trying to figure out their symptoms...so when someone comes in and presents like that, you're doing an investigation. You're trying to get a picture of what's going on with this person, and that's the same thing we do," he says.

Silence.

"Do I think that you're one of these guys who goes around doing this stuff all the time? No. Unless I'm wrong."

Silence.

"I know you're a good guy because you were going to swear that oath. You work in a home for people with intellectual disabilities. You're a good guy. I'm sure if you could rewind the clock right now, you would. What would you do? You'd change the whole thing, right?"

There's a knock at the door.

It's breakfast.

Allison continues, pulling out some photos of Taylor Samson and his brother, Connor. He proceeds to read Sandeson a post taken from Connor's Facebook page.

"There was a little boy inside the man who is my brother. Oh how I hated that little boy when I was one also, and how I loved him too at the same time. If anyone has seen or heard from my brother, Taylor, please let me or my mother know."

Then Allison tries to turn the tables, asking Sandeson to imagine how he would feel if his girlfriend went missing.

"Is she okay now?" Sandeson asks. "I know they picked her up."

"Yes, she's fine," Allison responds, before returning to his narrative.

"People make mistakes. Do we think that this was something that was set up ten times in a row, ten different people? No. You're a good person. Do you maybe buy some weed once in a while and sell some weed? Yeah."

Allison explains that he knows about weed, he used to be in the Guns and Gangs unit. He says lots of people sell weed for whatever reason. "But, Will, the difference here is that when most people meet up, one person doesn't go missing."

Silence.

"In your backpack you had money in there. You know what else is in there too, right?"

Still nothing.

"Will, you're at a crossroads right now. One way is going to take you in a certain direction, the other way is going to take you in a direction you don't want to go."

Silence.

"You're a mess. Did you sleep last night?"

Sandeson shakes his head.

"Not a wink," reiterates Allison.

He tells Sandeson that he had trouble sleeping because he's a good guy. "The bad guys, the monsters, Will, they have no trouble sleeping. You know why? Because they don't care. They don't care what they did or who they did it to."

Allison is trying to be his friend. "Will, you know I'm not lying to you. I'm not trying to trick you." No matter the tactic, nothing gets William Sandeson talking, not even Allison's repeated questions as to whether he's a monster.

"I want to help, but I just want to talk to the lawyer first," Sandeson says.

Allison explains that he's already had that opportunity.

"Twenty pounds of weed, that's a lot of money, right?" Allison asks, although he already knows the answer. Police estimated its worth at $90,000.

"But for what happened, do you think twenty pounds of weed is worth that? What's your heart tell you? Your heart tells you, William, that 2 million pounds of weed is not worth that, right?"

Sandeson again says that he just wants a lawyer to help him articulate what he needs to say.

"Something you got to remember is that if you tell the truth, you don't have to remember. Ever."

Sandeson agrees, pointing out that his dad says there's no such thing as a good liar because no one has a perfect memory.

Allison reminds him that the interview is being recorded, so if he can't remember his story two months from now, police will still have the tape.

"Saturday morning, did you wake up saying that you were going to be involved in a big racket? You know what I'm saying? Did you wake up, *boom!* 'I think I'm going to do some crazy stuff tonight?'"

Sandeson is silent. Allison notes he's crying.

"Are you concerned about the trafficking?"

"Not as much as I'm concerned about finding Taylor."

"Well then, why don't you tell us what happened?"

"I don't know how much help I can be, and how much it's going to hurt me."

"What the police see, what we think happened, that may not be the way it happened, and, Will, you need to speak up and say what the heck happened."

Sandeson is showing his intelligence, asking why he can't speak to a lawyer. Allison tells him again that he already has. Sandeson says the lawyer told him not to say anything and he continues asking questions about what will happen if he remains silent and how long he can be held, but Allison is undeterred.

"Will, what happened to Taylor? Is he alive?"

Sandeson just stares ahead. Allison is speaking calmly, almost sympathetically. It's as though he thinks he's about to make a breakthrough.

"Tell me what happened. Was there other people involved?"

But Sandeson still isn't talking.

"Is Taylor alive? You know the answer to that."

Sandeson shakes his head. "I don't know." A lie.

It's now 11:15 in the morning on Wednesday. The interrogation has been under way for just over an hour and nothing has been achieved.

"Will, if there's ever a time in your life when it's time to do the right thing, it's right now. It is right now. Will, you're telling me you want to help him. Well, what's holding you back right now? We need to find out—"

Sandeson interrupts him, "As soon as possible, I know." He's crying harder now.

Allison presses on. "Was it just you and him, William? These are questions that are not difficult to answer."

Sandeson is looking at the floor.

"Did somebody force you to do this?"

There's a knock on the door, and someone passes in Kleenex. Will Sandeson is hunched over with his head in his hands.

"William, if you were in my shoes—" Allison starts.

Sandeson interrupts him again. "I'd be so mad at me for not talking."

Allison says he's not mad.

"I'd be so mad and frustrated," says Sandeson. "I wouldn't understand."

Allison becomes firm. "You know that something happened Saturday night, Will. Is there a chance he's still alive?"

"I think so."

"You're telling me you think he's still alive, well then you better start talking. Doctors are logical people. Do you not see the logic in this whole thing?"

Sandeson blows his nose.

"Will, what happened? Did it have to do with the home invasion a couple of nights before that?"

The invasion was further explored at trial with the victim, an acquaintance of both Sandeson and Samson, providing dramatic testimony, but police said they determined it had nothing to do with what happened to Taylor Samson. What did happen and why was never really resolved.

Sandeson only continues his sobbing.

"[Samson] dropped off some stuff to your buddy and then all of a sudden there was a home invasion."

Silence.

"What happened, Will? Who are you trying to protect?"

"Me, I guess," he sobs.

Now Allison reaches out to put his hand on the accused's shoulder. Whatever the intent, it seems to work. Sandeson starts talking.

SANDESON'S STORY

"Someone came in my house," Sandeson begins. He is still sobbing when he starts his story, one that becomes, in the telling, more elaborate and implausible.

"When Taylor was there?" Allison asks.

Sandeson nods.

"Okay, who came in your house?" Allison asks.

"I don't know."

"Okay, what happened when they came in?"

"They were wearing masks. One of them had a gun, just one of them. We were sitting at the kitchen table. We were counting the money."

Allison pulls his hand away. Sandeson is talking. This is what he wants.

"The door wasn't locked, so they just came in. I tried to run to my room 'cause I was on the far side of the table. I got hit on the back of the head. I heard more fighting. They were telling me to stay down, and I knew they had a gun. And all it was next door was just loud music." He looks up at the officer, before continuing, "I just stayed down. They all left at the same time, I think. There was a lot of blood."

Sandeson stops to blow his nose. He is sobbing hard and appears to be struggling to breathe.

Allison takes the opportunity to continue questioning. "So you said when they first came in, they hit you and him with the gun?"

"No, he was closer to the door, and I tried to run into my room, and then they hit me."

Allison's voice is softening again. "And where did he hit you?"

"In the back of the head."

"Okay, and what did you say he hit you with?"

"I don't know, it felt, like, lumpy."

"Did you go down right away?"

"No, like, I turtled and crouched, and they just kept screaming, 'Get down,' and I tried to flatten out and then I got kicked in the head. And he was fighting, I'm sure he was fighting and it was just this scuffle."

"How long were they there at your apartment?"

Sandeson cries and shakes his head, as though he's trying to figure out the answer. He eventually tells the officer he doesn't know. "They didn't even take all the money," he says. "What was bloody they just left in blood, so I put it in a bag and cleaned it, and I cleaned the blood."

"You cleaned the money, you mean? Cleaned the blood off the money?"

"No, no," says Sandeson, almost hysterical. "The bloody money's in that bag."

Allison tells Sandeson he hasn't been in his apartment and asks him about the layout. Sandeson offers to draw it. "There's a long hallway," he says as he begins drawing on the back of a file folder. "There's two doors here." He continues for a couple of minutes, drawing and mumbling to himself. Then, "The weed's in a sack over by Taylor."

Allison jumps in: "The weed's in a sack? Like what do you mean?"

"Huge, like the biggest bag I've ever seen. I don't know if it was a hockey bag, but the biggest thing I've ever seen."

"So you said, they came in. Who's *they*?" Allison asks.

"I don't know," Sandeson responds, somewhat exasperated. "The guy with the gun was probably six feet. They were all in black, like black jeans. I only counted—it was three when I went down—I don't know if there were more."

"Okay."

"'Cause there was a lot of noise."

Allison wants to know how much money was on the table. Sandeson tells him there was $40,000 that the two planned to exchange for the twenty pounds of weed in the bag.

"Who knew that you and Taylor were meeting up?"

"No one should of."

"You know what I'm saying, for someone to randomly come into your place—"

"Right in the middle," says Sandeson, filling in the blank.

"Right in the middle of something like this," agrees Allison, the first sign he's not really buying Sandeson's story.

"How long were they there with Taylor?"

"It felt like forever, and I didn't get up until it was quiet."

"Which way did they go?"

"They went through the door. I don't know if he chased them or if they took him, but there was blood on the floor and money in the blood."

"So they just went right back out this way?" Allison says, referring to the drawing again.

"They had to," Sandeson replies, although he would later declare that door wasn't the only entrance to his apartment.

"Do you have surveillance in here? Video surveillance?"

"I put cameras in, but they don't record."

Wrong.

"They don't record, hey?"

Sandeson shakes his head. "They're shitty," he says, explaining that he put them in after his friend was robbed. He goes on to say that he's already put in complaints about the system not working, that it's supposed to record for two days without interruption, but it's been recording over itself every twenty minutes. Either Sandeson is lying or he doesn't know how to operate his own equipment—the system did not record over itself and it would become very useful for police.

"The thing about it—those things are like a computer hard drive," Allison explains, "So you know, you can go back in, chances are it's probably on there. They're actually checking it out, maybe even right now. So is that video going to show us pretty much what you told me?"

"Who goes up the hallway and who goes down the hallway," says Sandeson.

"Will, are you telling me the truth about everything?"

He nods, "I'm telling the truth," but it's barely decipherable through the sobbing.

"Why should I believe you?"

"Because I just told you everything."

"Would there be blood anywhere else?"

"From me walking around probably—I don't know—I tried to clean it."

"Where else did you try and clean?"

"I walked into my room. I walked into the bathroom to wash my hands. I took a shower. I didn't go into my roommate's room."

"Did you buy a new curtain for your bathroom?"

"Yes."

"What'd you do with the old one?"

"Threw it out." The reason Sandeson threw out the shower curtain would become a point of interest during his trial.

"Right. Will, are you being truthful with me about everything?" Sandeson nods.

"'Cause in everything that you say there's a certain element of truth, but sometimes there's some things that are left out."

"I admitted everything. Ask more questions if I don't have enough detail."

At this point, Allison reminds Sandeson that as part of the investigation they'll be speaking with a lot of other people.

Sandeson bows his head, gaze to the floor.

"Look at him," Allison says, reaching for a photo of Taylor and his brother, previously discarded on the floor of the interrogation room.

Sandeson looks away, crying.

"William." Allison points to the image of Taylor now sitting on Sandeson's knees.

"I know," he sobs. "I don't know." Sandeson looks right into the officer's eyes and continues crying.

"Don't make me think you're a monster, bud. Tell me the truth."

The two become engaged in a silent standoff, until the officer finally speaks. "You know where Taylor is."

"I don't know where he is!" Sandeson exclaims.

"Your body language is telling me something totally different than what you're shaking your head. In fact, sometimes you're actually nodding when you mean to be shaking. Where do you think he is?"

Allison makes contact again, placing a hand on Sandeson's shoulder.

"Don't overthink it. Where do you think he is?"

"I'm trying. I've been trying to think, okay!"

"In your heart, where do you think he's at?"

"I think someone took him."

"Where did they take him?"

"I don't know where they took him. I don't know who took him. I don't know who came in. I don't know. I tried to find out where he got his stuff from."

"Here's the thing, Will, listen to me for a second. I want you to think about something here. How long was he at your apartment before this happened?"

"Not long."

"Around two o'clock in the morning, you started sending him texts, 'Hey man this isn't cool.' Right?"

The officer is suggesting Sandeson sent the texts to cover his tracks, to make it look like Samson was still alive, when he knew full well the texts would never be answered.

"So you start trying to cover up what happened. Just listen to me," Allison says.

"I'm listening. I'm listening. I'm listening," Sandeson replies.

"So within a few hours, you're trying to cover up what happened. You go, you buy a new shower curtain, you clean up, right?"

"'Cause I'm scared."

"Do you see what I'm saying to you here, Will? What I'm saying to you is that your story is missing some pieces, some big pieces."

Sandeson's body is heaving with emotion, but he says nothing.

"What happened to the dope?"

"I dunno—same thing that happened to the money."

"Which was what?"

"It's gone."

Another lie. Sandeson knows exactly where the money and the drugs are.

"Here's a very simple question for you—when he left your apartment, was he alive? Yes or no?"

"I don't know."

Allison is slow and deliberate. "Will, when Taylor left your apartment was he dead or alive? Because it makes a huge difference."

"I don't know."

"Okay, well what do you know, Will? Do you know who these three people were?"

"No," he barely whispers.

"There wasn't three people was there?"

"Yes! There were."

Allison is adamant that if there were three people Sandeson had to know who they were, but Sandeson insists he does not know. Sandeson mentions an interview he had done the day before with a different investigator, Sergeant Charla Keddy. At that time, he was a witness, not a suspect.

"Why'd you give a version of events then that's totally different?" Allison asks.

Sandeson had told the first officer he was supposed to meet up with Taylor Samson that night to buy a small amount of marijuana, but that Samson didn't show up.

"I was scared."

Sandeson is now rocking in his chair with his hands clasped behind his head.

"You're a very intelligent man trying to make a version of events fit with what you think we have found. That's not how it works."

But the officer still seems to have faith in Sandeson, or at least that's what he wants him to believe. He explains there are different kinds of people—some calculated and cunning, others just scared because they made a mistake and got tangled up in something that wasn't supposed to go that way.

"Did you not have enough money?" he questions. "What really happened? I don't see any bumps on your head."

Nothing is working.

Allison pulls out the Hippocratic Oath again. He begins reciting, "'...the joy of healing those who seek my help.'"

"Did Taylor cry out for help? Did you hear him?" Allison's head is only inches from Sandeson's at this point. "Because if there was a big man, six foot five, two hundred and twenty pounds, being taken somewhere he doesn't want to go, he'd be doing some screaming, right?"

He pauses again.

"Unless of course he couldn't scream."

The silence stretches on.

Allison tries to appeal to Sandeson's humanity, saying he knows he wants to help Taylor's family and asking him to imagine what his own family would be going through if he were the one missing.

"The worst part for the families, Will, is the not knowing. I'm sure they have no idea what we found in that apartment, or what we found in your knapsack," he explains, pointing out Samson has now been missing for three and a half days.

William Sandeson is unmoving, bent over, his face shielded.

After three hours of interrogation, Corporal Jody Allison is not getting the confession he's seeking.

Allison leaves the room.

When Sandeson is alone, he tucks the photos of Taylor Samson and his brother Connor inside the file folder. Then he sits quietly, picking at his fingers. Eventually, he begins to pace in the tiny room. He rubs a shoulder injury, which the police would also question him about, then lies on the floor for more than thirty minutes.

When Allison returns, he confronts Sandeson with photos from his apartment, telling him that what the Ident team has found doesn't match his story.

"I'm not sure what the plan was at the beginning of it, but I don't think it turned out quite the way that it was supposed to. If you're the ringleader in this, Will, if you're the master planner, that's one thing. If your part in this was something different, then that's quite another."

Then he starts questioning Sandeson about the others involved, explaining that, whoever they are, they'll drag him down with them. "It's a race to the finish line, so I think it's time that you reassessed what you told me."

But he doesn't.

"Are you the mastermind in this?"

Sandeson shakes his head.

"Did you know that your phone pings off cellphone towers even when you're not making and receiving calls?" Police would use those pings to retrace Sandeson's steps over the last couple of days.

"When you said you cleaned up, how good a job do you think you did?" Allison asks, flipping through a stack of photos he's holding.

"Probably awful."

"Awful, yeah, I would say."

"You have a firearm registered to you, right?"

"Yes."

"Did you ever shoot anything with it?"

"Targets."

"Do you know where your firearm is right now?"

"I don't know if you have it in your possession or not."

"Would we have it in our possession if we searched your apartment?"

"Yeah, it's stored in my safe."

Allison resumes flipping through photos of Sandeson's apartment. "What'd they find in the bathroom?" He points to an image showing what looks like blood spatter. "What happened in there?"

He flips through more photos. "Look at this. There's still blood on the money, for God's sake, Will, there's blood on the money. That's blood money."

Sandeson sobs. He's shaking.

"If you were used in this to set this thing up then you gotta say, 'cause I'm having a hard time making the leap between somebody who wants to be a doctor, who helps out at group homes, to this happening. I'm having a hard time making that connection, so please explain to me how this happened, that you ended up in the middle of this crap."

Allison now clearly defines his role as "good cop," telling Sandeson that he's trying to explain to the other officers that he doesn't believe he is the ringleader. "This guy is a good guy, he's going to be a doctor, for Christ's sake," begging Sandeson to help him make the others understand.

The sobbing is intensifying rapidly.

"This is a bad situation you were put in. You were forced." Allison tells Sandeson he will feel so much better once he talks. "You've got so much weight on you right now, so much weight."

Allison pulls his chair even closer to Sandeson.

"Get a grip on yourself, okay. Listen to me, listen to my voice. Calm down, okay. Take a couple of deep breaths. We'll go through this together."

Allison acknowledges Sandeson is trying to talk but can't because he's sobbing so hard.

"I think I'm going to pass out."

The officer tells him to sit up, acknowledging he's under a lot of stress.

"Tell me who was there besides you. Your next-door neighbour, was he there?"

Sandeson doesn't answer the question, but his next-door neighbour would become a key player in his case.

"Will, I think it's time, this is the moment of truth here, bud. I think it's time that you set the record straight here right now."

When Sandeson says nothing, Allison presents him with still photos from his home-surveillance system, the one the student thought recorded over itself after twenty minutes. Not so.

"Do you recognize that as being from yours?"

"Yes."

"And that's Taylor coming in, right?"

"Yes."

"So why don't we start from the beginning. How about we start from when he first goes in the door."

Allison reminds Sandeson that the police are also talking to the other people seen on the video from his home DVR cameras.

"The thing about it, Will, is that you're the guy that texts him to come over."

Then Allison notes the time on the surveillance stills. It is 10:26 P.M. on August 15, 2015, when Taylor Samson walks into Sandeson's apartment, carrying a big black duffle bag.

"I think you know exactly what happened to Taylor, right, Will? And I can tell by the way that you're acting right now that you feel horrible."

The crying starts again.

"When it was set up, was there intention to hurt him? To injure him? Were you told that they were gonna injure him?"

"No."

He puts his hand on Sandeson's shoulder again, telling him that he knows he's scared, but now is his chance.

"I want you to have your story of what happened inside that apartment out before somebody else gets it out and paints you with a brush that you're some evil genius."

Allison has been talking for nearly six hours.

"Whatever happened wasn't done very professionally, if you ask me. This looks like a bunch of amateurs. I know you said that you cleaned up, but obviously you can tell that you didn't do a real good job." He notes there's blood on the table and chairs, the walls, and the money.

"Why don't you want to talk and tell me who else was there? Unless there was nobody else there." It's the first time he's mentioned the possibility Sandeson acted alone, that he may not be buying the story. "You don't have to say what they did or what they didn't do. Just who else was there with you?"

Sandeson rocks back and forth, his hands clasped between his legs now.

Allison explains that he can only give him so many opportunities to talk, and they're running out. He reaches for his stack of photos, flips to the images of Sandeson's phone, and begins reciting text messages Sandeson sent to Taylor Samson:

"I'm walking out now."

And later, "This isn't cool man. You said you'd be right back. Want that stuff."

"Do you know how bad this looks? Do you know how bad this looks?" Allison demands, before returning to the texts.

"Yo man, Taylor's gone missing. Like he's being treated as a missing person by the police," Allison is reading a text someone else sent to Sandeson. "When's the last time you talked to him?"

"Saw him Thursday to check out sample. Then nothing," Sandeson responded in the texts. A lie. The video is proof Sandeson saw Samson on Saturday night.

"Shit man, that's scary," said his friend.

"Do you know how bad this looks?" Allison implores again. "Do you understand the predicament you're in, Will?

"Yes," Sandeson whispers, nodding with his head bowed.

"So why is it that you can't explain what happened? Why is it that you can't say who else was there? Why is it that you can't tell me where Taylor is? Who did he leave with, Will? Will, Will, who did he leave with?" Allison repeats it over and over like a mantra. It doesn't work.

"Was it just gonna be a drug rip and then he got mad? That's all it was?" demands Allison. "Or did you even know it was gonna be a drug rip?"

Sandeson begins to get emotional again, and the officer pleads with him, "Stay with me...did he throw the first punch? He's a big man. Tell me about how it started. Did you start it?"

Sandeson is now sobbing again.

"[Are] these guys going to harm somebody if you tell? Or are they really close to you and you don't want to say?"

Sandeson has now been under interrogation for seven hours.

"Let's get the people that fucked your life up. Who was it? Do you want to tell me what happened?"

"Yes," he whispers. But it doesn't come right away.

"Why don't you tell me? Do you think I'm going to think you're evil or something like that?"

"I want to say but I can't prove it."

"Don't worry about proving it. Who else was there? That's not for you to prove. That's for us to prove."

Sandeson cries harder.

"Okay, let's start with this—were they male?"

He nods.

"Okay, was one a black male or a white male, or Hispanic?"

No response.

"Was there more than one male there? How about that?"

"Yes."

"Okay, was there two males there? Okay, so there's you, Taylor, and the two other males, so there's four people altogether?"

No response, but Allison forges on. He seems to be getting somewhere.

"Now, these other two males, are they friends of yours?"

Sandeson shakes his head *no*.

"Let me put it this way, are they associates of yours?"

He shakes his head *no* again.

"Okay, but you know who they are but you don't want to say their names. Are they associated to you through drug transactions? How about let's start with one name? Just one name."

But the limited progress has come to a halt.

"Did you ever hear tell of the saying, 'hen's teeth. It's like pulling hen's teeth?' Very hard to get information," says Allison. "I'm trying to understand how this happened."

BAD COP

Then there's a knock on the door. Allison leaves and another officer enters. This is different. He's not patient, like Corporal Allison, but firm, almost angry, from the outset. He's physically bigger too, tall, with a commanding presence.

"Will, remember me—Detective Constable [Roger] Sayer? I spoke to you last night. Remember that?"

"Yup."

"I told you last night that I was one of the lead investigators on this file, and I've been here all day, all night, all week, okay. I've been watching you all day, and you've done nothing since I first saw you yesterday but lie. I told you that evidence would show that, and it has been doing it all day, and we haven't stopped collecting evidence. Do you understand that, Will?"

"Yes."

"Have not stopped. And you sit in here and you keep going on and lying and lying and lying, and you don't need to. You need to get past that. That needs to stop." He points to the growing pile of photos and documents on the floor and explains that so far the evidence disproves everything Sandeson has told police.

"Blood evidence. People come in and take twenty pounds of weed and $40,000 and they leave you what—a damage deposit? Not to mention the stack of twenties that's found in your bathroom underneath the garbage bag in your garbage can. Will, you need to start to get your head right, 'cause you think all this bullshit you're laying down, you think you're smarter than everybody that's working on this, you're making a very drastic mistake. Drastic."

Sandeson is quiet, listening intently.

"Jody believes in you. I tried to tell him 'cause I was in here last night and I saw what was what, but he believes that what you're trying to say is true. I don't."

It's clear Sayer is playing the "bad cop" in the "good cop/bad cop" scenario.

Sayer picks up a photo. "There's blood on this table that somebody cleaned up and, like they always do because they all think they're smarter than they are, you wiped the top but don't think of the side. What's that going to be tested for?"

"DNA," Sandeson barely squeaks out.

"DNA," Sayer confirms.

"More blood," announces Sayer. "Blood on the chair. There's blood in your bathroom, on the floorboards, on the curtain. Your own words were that it happened in your kitchen area. How'd all that blood get in your bathroom?"

Sandeson keeps his eyes to the floor.

"Will, look at me. You're in here crying and going on, and you know what happened. There is nothing that I have seen in here today that suggests anybody showed up at that place. Nothing. That video runs for over an hour. No one comes, no one leaves. Then your system is turned off. If you think that people are that stupid, you're fooling yourself."

Sandeson is still silent.

"Listen, buddy, you don't have to be Colombo to figure out that between 11:33 and 1 A.M., when that system was turned off, is when he left—however he left."

Sayer tells Sandeson they've also seized his car. "How much of that do you think we need to find to get DNA," he asks, smacking a photograph of blood.

"Less than a drop," Sandeson replies meekly.

"Yup," Sayer responds. "And when we check your car, what if his DNA's in there? What's your story then? These mystery people made you drive him away?"

And then the interrogation takes another turn. "You're a liar, cold, calculating, and lying." He jabs at a photograph again, this one of Taylor Samson. "Where is this man? Where is he, Will? What happened in your apartment?"

Sandeson sniffles and bows his head.

"Don't put your head down, man. Where is he?" He thrusts the photo of Samson under Sandeson's eyes. "What did you do to this man?"

He runs down the evidence police already have against him.

"You're lying, man. You've been lying all day." It's now coming up on six o'clock in the evening.

"When you're in this room with people who are innocent, they kick and scream, bud."

Sandeson hangs his head.

"I heard him ask you a hundred times, 'Who's the name?' You crying and blowing in the Kleenex," he mocks, "like you're some kind of victim. You're a predator, bud."

Sayer's voice is aggressive, but slow and deliberate.

"I want to bring that man home to his family. Where is he?"

There is no crying now.

"You're done, bud. Done. There's no going past that, but you can do something right."

Sandeson still says nothing.

There's a knock on the door. Sayer gathers up the photos he's spread over the floor of the interrogation room. He places the one of Taylor and his brother on the chair and sets it in front of William Sandeson. "I'm going to leave and watch you push that away." He walks out.

GOOD COP

Jody Allison is back in the room, playing "good cop." Sandeson is calm now. Allison wants to know more about the people who supposedly came into his apartment.

"Can you tell what time they showed up?"

Without hesitation, he responds, "Just after eleven."

"Just after eleven?"

Then he backtracks. "No, sorry, just after Taylor got there but they came through, they were in Dylan's room." Dylan Zinck-Selig was Sandeson's roommate, although he was rarely at the apartment, choosing instead to stay with his girlfriend.

"They were in Dylan's room?" Allison asks.

Sandeson explains that there's a window in Zinck-Selig's bedroom that can be used to access a roof where they used to keep a barbecue. Back with the good cop, Sandeson is telling his story, freely adding details.

"So somebody could have went in through there?" Allison asks.

Sandeson nods.

"Did you know that they were in there?"

"Yes."

"Okay, so what was the plan supposed to be that you were aware of?"

"A scare tactic."

"To scare him? Like for what purpose?"

"I don't know, to scare him out of dealing. I know he owed money."

"Okay, so these two guys that were in Dylan's room, so when you told me about—" Allison trails off.

"It's not the truth when I said they came through the front door," Sandeson finishes the statement.

"Okay, so tell me what happened when these two guys come out."

Sandeson stops now, bowing his head again.

"Was it the same as what you told me before?"

"Not exactly." He shakes his head. "I still retreated towards my room."

"And then what happened?"

"They were just talking to Taylor. Taylor didn't get up because they had a gun on him."

"Then what happened?"

"Then I shut off the surveillance camera."

"So you shut it off yourself?"

He nods.

"Okay. Was that because they asked you to do that?"

He nods again.

"So when they got you to do that, what happened next?"

A long silence ensues, and finally, "They put Taylor in the bag with the weed."

An outrageous twist.

"They put him in the bag with the weed?"

He nods.

"Okay, what was going on with him when they put him in there? Like, was he dead or alive?"

Sandeson sinks his head into his hands again.

"'Cause a minute ago they were talking to him, right?"

"There was a gunshot. I didn't see what happened. Then there was a lot of blood. They put him in the bag and then went out."

"Okay, so you didn't see—how do you know that they put him in the bag?"

"They left with the bag and he wasn't there."

"How many gunshots did you hear?" Allison asks, pulling up a chair again.

"One."

"Now this bag, I remember you saying—"

Sandeson interrupts. "It was the biggest bag I've ever seen."

"Okay, so what kind of things are they saying to you when this is going on?"

"They weren't talking to me."

"No, but can you hear them? What are they saying to Taylor?"

"He was done."

"So they were saying to him, like you know, 'You're done,' and what was he saying back to them?"

"That he had money coming, like this was supposed to be a deal for both of us."

"What happened to the weed that was in that bag?"

"It stayed in the bag."

Another lie.

"And what did they do then?"

"They walked out the door."

"They went through the regular door, like down the stairs?"

He nods. "I didn't follow them. I started cleaning."

"When you saw these guys, just pick one of them and describe him to me."

"Six-footish, dressed all in black. They had like a Morphsuit face, like black Morphsuits."

"Morphsuits? I'm not sure what you mean by that."

Sandeson explains it's a spandex bodysuit like members of the Blue Man Group wear.

"Did you see anything in their hands or on their hands?"

"They only had one gun between the two." Remember, Sandeson first told Allison there were three intruders.

"Can you describe it to me, because I know you're familiar with guns?"

"It looked like mine except it was all black. The slide on mine's silver."

"So your gun is a Smith & Wesson gun. Are you familiar with the different types of guns?"

"Not at all. I went in and asked for a rookie gun, and that's what they gave me."

"Okay, describe the other person to me."

"He was bigger, like six-three or four."

"I know you didn't see the shot, but where was he hit?"

Sandeson reaches around and rubs the area around the back of his neck.

"And he was sitting in the chair when that happened?"

He nods.

"So you heard the shot, then did you look out? You're in your bedroom, you said. What did you do then?"

"I...I shouted out. Shouted to them."

"And what did they say?"

"Like, 'never mind, mind your own business. And you can clean up and you can keep that dirty money.'"

"Okay, so what did you do then?"

"I cleaned up. I mopped the blood with a Swiffer WetJet."

It must be enough.

Allison leaves the room. When he comes back, he tells Sandeson he's arresting him for murder. After more than nine hours of interrogation, a young man pledging to save lives has been accused of taking a life.

CHAPTER 2
SCENE OF
THE CRIME

When Taylor Samson left his South Street apartment and walked around the corner to 1210 Henry Street the night of August 15, he had no idea what he was getting into. His girlfriend, Mackenzie Ruthven, later said he told her he was going a couple of houses down and would be right back. She didn't think anything of it. He had done it so many times before.

Minutes later, he's seen on surveillance video walking into the Henry Street complex where Will Sandeson lived. It's a bright yellow building consisting of three apartments above an Asian grocery store. There's a giant dragon and Chinese symbols painted on the exterior of the building, graffiti scrawled beneath them, and a laundromat next door.

Halifax is a coastal capital that offers the amenities of most major cities while maintaining the slower pace of life by the sea. Amalgamating with surrounding municipalities in 1996, the Halifax Regional Municipality (HRM) now has a population of approximately four hundred thousand.

Home to Canada's East Coast Navy, the Department of National Defence is Halifax's single largest employer. CFB

Halifax is Canada's largest naval base. Other major employers are the Port of Halifax, the Halifax Shipyard, owned by Irving Shipbuilding and currently building Canada's next fleet of warships after being awarded a $25 billion contract by the federal government, and Dalhousie University, which both William Sandeson and Taylor Samson attended.

The South End neighbourhood, where both students lived, is heavily populated with students, but this is not a typical student neighbourhood. Located on the southern half of a peninsula that juts out into the Atlantic Ocean, South End Halifax is a residential area home to some of Halifax's wealthiest families.

In 1918, a major railway line was built through deep rock for several kilometres, paralleling the shore of the Northwest Arm. Another line had been under construction when the Halifax Explosion of 1917 devastated the city. A French cargo ship laden with explosives collided with a Norwegian vessel in Halifax Harbour, killing an estimated two thousand people, injuring nine thousand more, and causing widespread destruction in the city's North End. The new railway line through the South End was rushed to completion to accommodate the unexpected disaster. One result of the blasting process has been to geographically isolate parts of the peninsula by creating secluded areas and opportunities for wealthy and exclusive neighbourhoods to develop.

The South End has become the most prosperous region of Halifax. In 2014, *Canadian Business* magazine named it the number -one wealthiest neighbourhood in Nova Scotia, with the average household income at $225,995 a year and the average price of a home at $1.03 million.

The South End is not only home to Dalhousie, but two other universities, Saint Mary's University and the University of King's College.

Constable Robin Sherwood is the Halifax Regional Police's community-response officer for the area around the universities. He's also responsible for the force's Operation Fallback, a program introduced in 2004 that involves stepped-up enforcement as a direct response to quality-of-life issues for people who live in the South End when the students come flooding back in September.

"As far as I see it, the students are a part of our city and they act as a vibrant part of the city," says Sherwood in an interview. "It's just that sometimes we have to remind them about some of their behaviours at nighttime that could disturb others."

Most of the issues Sherwood's team responds to in the fall have to do with noise complaints, public intoxication, and underage drinking. He says the number of tickets issued for noise complaints has declined significantly over the years since Operation Fallback was introduced, but the number of tickets issued to students for drinking has remained consistent.

Three months after Taylor Samson was killed, in November 2015, police were called to a Dalhousie residence after a nineteen-year-old international student from China died of alcohol poisoning. Her parents are now suing the university.

Founded in 1818, Dalhousie now has nineteen thousand students from 115 different countries, according to the university's website. Thirty-three per cent of students come to Halifax from surrounding Nova Scotia communities, small towns like Amherst and Truro, from which Taylor Samson and William Sandeson hailed, respectively.

The university offers 180 different degree programs and boasts it has had 90 Rhodes scholars. In 2017 it had 999 professors, and more than 90 percent of them had a PhD or doctorate.

Dal is proud of its internationally recognized medical school, declaring that it has the most up-to-date medical school curriculum in Canada. At the time of this writing, there were 436 medical students enrolled in the four-year MD program, with more than 91 per cent hailing from the Maritimes. Dal's website also states that while most doctors in Canada's Maritime provinces were educated at Dal, its graduates can also be found caring for people throughout the country and around the world.

As the school prepares for the beginning of its third century, it plans to use the anniversary to build awareness and enhance its reputation. Some might say it could really use the boost.

When William Sandeson was charged with first-degree murder in August 2015, Dal had already been through a tumultuous period. It had been eight months since the Dal dentistry scandal made national headlines after male members of the class were revealed to have launched a sexist and misogynistic Facebook page about their female colleagues. The group was called the "Class of DDS 2015 Gentlemen," but the members were anything but gentlemen. In December 2014 school officials were provided with dozens of screenshots identifying women in the class. CBC Nova Scotia also obtained the screenshots and published many of them. One post in the group asked the question, "Who would you hate fuck?" and provided a poll that included photos of their female classmates. The posts also included jokes about using chloroform, a colourless, sweet-smelling liquid, which can be used by dentists during root-canal procedures, and has also been used by various criminals, including serial killers Paul Bernardo and Karla Homolka, to knock out their victims.

In the Dal case, the CBC reported, the words, "Does this rag smell like chloroform to you??" were superimposed on one photo. Just over a week after the story broke, the university's president, Richard Florizone, announced that the young women involved had decided to proceed with a restorative-justice process that was already under way. That caused an outcry and hundreds of people marched and protested, demanding the students be expelled. The controversy even forced the temporary closure of the school's dental clinic. In May 2015, a report on the restorative-justice process found a culture of unprofessionalism within the dentistry faculty. All of the students involved in the scandal ended up graduating with their class.

Less than a week after William Sandeson was arrested in 2015, another Dal med student would be arrested after telling a psychiatrist he planned to kill twenty people, including the school's associate dean of undergraduate medical education and her daughter. Stephen Tynes's psychiatrist went to police after a session in which he mused about a mass shooting. Those criminal charges were later withdrawn when the Crown determined the evidence wasn't as strong as initially thought. They were replaced with a peace-bond hearing.

Tynes was also charged with unauthorized possession of a prohibited device, after police seized 1,834 rounds of ammunition for rifles, a Russian SKS rifle, a Henry Golden Boy .22-calibre rifle, a banana clip for a rifle, a baggie with three spring clips and bore cleaner, two ammunition boxes, a firearms acquisition card, and a gun club card. He eventually pleaded guilty to the weapons charge and was given a conditional discharge for that offence.

Tynes had been previously charged for killing a cat, but that charge was also withdrawn. He has since been charged with sexual assault. That charge is also working its way through the court system.

Another of the university's professional schools also attracted bad publicity. Eight months after Sandeson's arrest, in April 2016, a recent graduate of Dal's Schulich School of Law was charged with the second-degree murder of his girlfriend, Halifax entrepreneur and yoga instructor Kristin Johnston. Thirty-four-year-old Nicholas Butcher stabbed Johnston to death, then cut off his own hand with a power saw before calling 911 himself.

Butcher was convicted of second-degree murder in April 2018.

The university has since re-evaluated how students are admitted to its prestigious medical school for the first time in ten years. As the Sandeson case particularly progressed toward a trial that would captivate the city of Halifax and much of the province of Nova Scotia, people wondered how a cold-blooded killer could be accepted to medical school. Others expressed outrage when reporters associated him with the school.

"As a Dal med school graduate, I find it offensive that William Sandeson is called a Dal medical student," one person wrote to me via social media. "He was accepted but never attended and was therefore NOT a medical student."

"Referencing Sandeson as an 'Aspiring Doctor' is an outrage to the medical profession," another man Tweeted at me. "You grab a headline with a label that insults anyone who had put in the time and effort to earn the degree."

The fact remains, William Sandeson was a Dal medical student and was most certainly an aspiring doctor.

CHAPTER 3
WHO WAS TAYLOR SAMSON?

My Plan

1. *1ˢᵗ $100,000 + investment by the time I am 25*
2. *I will give back everything I can to those who deserve it and more*
3. *by the time I am 25*
4. *I will accumulate enough wealth early on so that I will never have to worry about money ever again.*
5. *I will Inovate [sic], develop and make the world a better place, as well as influence the lives of many*
6. *Before I die. (Hope to make it to 30. haha)*

The "Plan" was found scribbled on a piece of graph paper in Taylor Samson's bedroom after he disappeared. According to his friends, the note says a lot about who Samson really was: his entrepreneurial spirit, his desire to change the cycle of poverty within which he was raised, and his passion for helping others. The last line, no doubt meant as a joke by an invincible twenty-something, is now hauntingly heartbreaking. Samson wouldn't make it to thirty. He wouldn't make it to twenty-three.

Taylor Dean James Samson was born on March 2, 1993. The family was living in Tantallon, a Halifax suburb, at the time. It was a beautiful day, despite the calendar having not yet turned to spring, so nice his mother missed a barbeque when she had to go to the hospital. It was a fast labour, less than two hours, before Taylor came into the world weighing seven pounds, fourteen and a half ounces, twenty-two inches long—his mother rattles off the statistics as though it were yesterday.

"Within six months, his doctor told me that he was going to be over six feet tall the way he was growing," says his mother, Linda Boutilier. And he was.

It's now the middle of summer 2017, and as we sit in her kitchen drinking coffee, she tells me she never thought she would have children. In fact, she didn't plan to have Taylor, but at thirty-two years old, she had been with his father, Dean Samson, for a couple of years and the news she was pregnant wasn't unwelcome either. Two years later she would go on to have another son, Connor, and the two boys could not have been more different.

Taylor never slept, he would be awake at 7 A.M. and not go to bed until 11 P.M., and he didn't sleep through the night until he was just over a year old. "He was too nosy," his mother laughs. Connor, on the other hand, slept like an angel and was always a quiet child.

Taylor, his mother says, was crawling at six months, walking by eight months, and running by ten months. "He was running all over the place, he was climbing chairs, he'd be up on the counter."

After being assessed as advanced for his age, Taylor began preschool early at the Peanut Butter Palace, at just three and a half years old. He loved animals as much as he loved other children, but for some reason, he was always a protector. His mother recounts a story from those early preschool days when Taylor witnessed another boy push a little girl he believed to be his girlfriend.

"Taylor punched him in the nose and gave him a nosebleed," his mother says. "That's when it started."

It could have been a sign of things to come. Taylor wanted to protect everyone in his life—his friends, his family, but most of all, his mother and his brother, who lives with autism.

"As much as they argued, if anyone ever came near Connor that would be it—Taylor would be standing right there, protecting him," Boutilier explains. Life was not always easy for the family and Taylor seemed to believe his hardship came with added responsibility.

He had just started school when his parents separated. He was five years old. When he was seven, Boutilier took the boys and moved to Amherst, a community two hundred kilometres northwest of Halifax, near the New Brunswick border, population just under ten thousand.

In 1872, the Intercolonial Railway of Canada constructed its main line from Halifax to Quebec through Amherst, leading to industrialization and numerous factories and mills, giving the town its nickname "Busy Amherst." These days, the town, like many others in Nova Scotia, is suffering from a declining population, but remains the retail hub for surrounding communities.

Boutilier trained as a certified nursing assistant (now known as a licensed practical nurse or LPN) and worked in geriatrics. She also has a diploma in business administration and microcomputers but disliked it and never worked in the field. For years she worked in a nursing home but says that got more difficult when she became a single mother because it was challenging to do shift work. On top of that, she had deteriorating discs in her back and there came a point when she could no longer handle the lifting required to do the job. For most of her children's childhoods she worked at Walmart and McDonald's, bringing in $24,000 a year, struggling to make ends meet.

It was a life she didn't want for her kids.

"When they were growing up, the first thing I always taught them, school is not done until you finish university or college.

You're not done at grade twelve. I put it in their heads for years because I didn't want them to end up struggling like I did."

For all of the challenges, she takes comfort in knowing she raised her sons to be kind, loving young men who treated people well. She recalls a day when Taylor slipped a five-dollar bill to a panhandler as they walked by. When she gave him a questioning look, he said, "Mom, I know what it's like to be hungry."

She starts to cry. "It was like I raised him right, you know?"

She says he didn't really know what it was like to be hungry.

"Sometimes there was whacks of groceries and other times I just couldn't afford to be out buying the steaks and expensive stuff, but you know, there was always something." And there was always something for everyone.

Described as a "community mom" by Taylor's friends, Boutilier's door was always open, literally never locked. Sometimes, as they got older, friends even slept there when Taylor wasn't home, and it wasn't unusual for him to come home ten minutes before supper with three other kids who hadn't yet eaten. "I had three pork chops, so I would have a piece of toast or a can of soup, while the rest of the kids all ate. I'd make goulash or something, just so they could all eat."

She doesn't think Taylor worried about money much as a child because he didn't understand it, but she does think he felt he had a responsibility to take care of her and his brother and recalls him telling her that he had to be the man of the house. He was twelve.

"I said, 'No you don't, you have to be a little boy and grow up.'"

It wasn't until he was around sixteen, she says, that he really started worrying.

His friend, Thomas McCrossin, who is also from Amherst but now lives in Halifax, has the same recollection. McCrossin is the son of Elizabeth Smith-McCrossin, a Progressive Conservative member of the Nova Scotia legislature, representing the area in which Taylor Samson grew up.

"I remember talking to him one night—we probably had drinks into us—and we were getting right passionate and talking about stuff, and he's like, 'Thomas, you have no idea what it's like to worry about whether or not you're gonna have heat or food.' That was what he was talking about back when he was fifteen or sixteen."

Boutilier says she got behind in bills so that Taylor could play baseball.

"Amherst was everything about baseball," Boutilier says. So, when Taylor was in grade one, his mother signed him up. He loved it.

Ryan Wilson met Taylor around that time. The two played on the all-star team together and became fast friends. "He brought me out of my shell. He introduced me to so many people," says Wilson, twenty-four at the time of this writing. "He helped me be a better friend and showed me how easy it was to be a friend to someone else as well."

From the time they were thirteen to seventeen years old, Wilson, who attended the trial with Linda and Connor, says he can't remember a weekend when one of them wasn't at the other's house.

"I was actually the first one out of all the guys to meet Dean. Nobody knew who Dean was. [Taylor] never spoke about him. I just didn't ask," he says, but then one day when they were around fifteen or sixteen years old, Taylor called him up and asked if he wanted to meet his dad. "I mean, sure, yeah, I'm not gonna say no to that, and he's like, 'Okay, well he lives in Cole Harbour.' I'm like, 'How are we getting there?' And he's like, 'I dunno. Do you know?' And I'm like, 'No.'" So they hitchhiked.

Taylor's mother didn't know about any of it until many years later. "I found out a lot of things years later," she chuckles, but in a way that makes it obvious she doesn't think it's funny. Not funny at all.

It was the last Christmas they had together, Taylor was home from university, and they sat and watched *Big Bang Theory* all day while a storm raged outside. "We just chatted and talked and talked and talked about everything," Boutilier recalls.

Then he asked her, "Mom, you remember that time when I went to Ryan's?" She hardly did. "Well we kind of didn't," he said, after he had jogged her memory, and then proceeded to explain that he and his friend had hitchhiked to his father's in Cole Harbour—a Halifax suburb best known as the hometown of NHL superstar Sidney Crosby—and camped out in his yard.

As Boutilier rushed on that they could have made arrangements and driven him there, Taylor said, "I wanted to go down and smoke a joint with my dad." She asked him why, the response painful to repeat. "He said, 'I wanted to make him proud of me,'" she sobs. "That's what he said."

Taylor's father says he doesn't recall the incident at all, and says he didn't smoke with Taylor until he became an adult.

Boutilier believes her son started smoking weed when he was around seventeen years old, after being diagnosed with an autoimmune liver disease and realizing he couldn't drink. His friends recall he may have been much younger.

McCrossin, who also met Taylor through baseball but didn't become a close friend until university, says Taylor was dealing when he was fourteen or fifteen. He admits he bought weed from Taylor, says pretty much everyone did.

His mother maintains he didn't start selling until the summer before he moved to Halifax to go to university. He had been working at Walmart and asked her if he could take the summer off. She told him that he could but warned she would not have extra money to fuel his fun. He agreed.

"Then he started to have a bit of money, and then you'd see a couple of people come in I didn't hardly know, so I figured he was selling a few grams." She confronted him, and he confirmed it was true, but only small amounts.

She didn't know he continued selling in Halifax, and didn't find out about it until his second year of school when he got sick and she ended up going to the city to spend a few days with him. Again she noticed people she didn't know coming and going. She still believed he was only selling small amounts, and while she doesn't smoke herself, she says many of her friends do.

"I grew up with most of my friends smoking, so to me it's not a big deal anyways. Most of them own their own businesses."

Still, she asked him to stop and even got into arguments with him about it. It was his education she was worried about, telling him, "You're going to get kicked out of university and everything you worked for is just going to be gone."

But it always came back to the money. Taylor couldn't make ends meet with just his student loan. "I actually got behind in my own rent to help him out because he was behind. That's when he started to sell drugs, because I couldn't afford it, he couldn't afford it," she pauses. "Then it got easier."

And when it got easier, Taylor could help his mom. When his brother Connor started his first job working at the lobster plant at Westmorland Fisheries in Cap-Pelé, New Brunswick, he needed steel-toed boots.

"We had the money for part of the boots. I was short like eighty bucks, and he had to start right away." Taylor sent them $100 to get the boots. But, she says, when Taylor's student loan didn't come through on time, she sent him money, and so they helped each other whenever they could.

TALL, DARK, AND HANDSOME

Despite his illegal recreational activity, or perhaps because of it, Taylor seemed to be thriving at university. He did well in class, had a girlfriend, and joined a fraternity.

While he wasn't a great student in high school, he loved physics and believed he could use it to change the world. He talked about getting his PhD, finding a cure for autoimmune disease, and solving the equation that would facilitate teleportation.

At six foot five, Samson was "tall, dark, and handsome" with a head of thick brown hair and a grin-splitting smile in nearly every picture. His good looks seemed to work for him. His friends say he had no problem attracting many girlfriends over the years.

At the time of his disappearance, he had been with Mackenzie Ruthven for six months, and his mother thought she was the one. Boutilier was excited because, while he had dated several, he had never brought a woman home to meet her. He brought Mackenzie home on Mother's Day and for his mother's birthday, and they all went out for supper.

Ruthven, who is from Harrow, a small community in southern Ontario on the shores of Lake Erie, was twenty-one in 2017 when she testified at the trial of the man accused of killing her boyfriend in the summer of 2015. She's a pretty, petite young woman with brown hair that hangs down past her waist.

The first time she met Samson's mother, Ruthven explained she was also working on a bachelor of science with plans to go to medical school, Boutilier recalls. "And I'm going, 'Oh my god, I'm gonna have a doctor in the family!' and Taylor's sitting there, 'Mom, you're embarrassing me,' and she's just laughing. I really really really liked her," says Boutilier, thinking back on the memory.

But Boutilier wasn't so sure about the fraternity. Taylor joined the Gamma Rho Chapter of Sigma Chi in his second year of university. The organization's website says its purpose is to cultivate, maintain, and accomplish the ideals of friendship, justice, and learning. His mother didn't understand it, believing he was nothing like the "nerdy" people she believed to be among the group.

"His honest words were, 'Mom, you don't realize how intelligent they are. I can learn so much from them,'" Boutilier says.

It was through the fraternity that Taylor would meet another close friend, Kaitlynne Lowe, who was a member of Alpha Gamma Delta, a sorority that says it is focused on scholarship, sisterhood, and philanthropy.

Lowe, who is now the president of the Dalhousie Association of Graduate Students, met Taylor during her second year at Dal at a party in January 2014. "He and I ended up talking the entire night and we just hung out," she says. "I had never felt so connected with a person so wholly. We jumped every conversation, everything from people that we commonly knew, what we liked to do and where we liked to go, to what we thought about life. It was a really impactful night."

Lowe attended both Will Sandeson's preliminary inquiry and his trial, with Taylor's mother and other friends. The preliminary inquiry, which determines whether there is enough evidence for the case to go to trial, was especially important to her. The details were subject to a publication ban, meaning members of the media could not report them, so Lowe sat in court, taking detailed notes that would help her explain what was happening to Taylor's family and friends who could not attend.

She insists their relationship was always platonic. In fact they were both dating other people. Still, just a couple of days after they met, she ended up celebrating her birthday with him.

"He didn't accept that my plan for my birthday was literally to work all day and then write an essay, so he had me over and we ordered Thai food and then we just hung out and watched Netflix. I was up 'til about 3 A.M. for an eight o'clock in the morning class."

The Gamma Rho Chapter in Halifax was Sigma Chi's 94th instalment and Canada's third. It is now one of the largest collegiate fraternities with undergraduate chapters at 241 universities and colleges. The fraternity's alumni include Brad Pitt, David Letterman, Tom Selleck, and the late Jack Layton, leader of Canada's New Democratic Party.

Samson had just moved into the chapter frat house on South Street in Halifax, a two-storey home with beige siding proudly displaying the frat's name and emblem on a bright blue sign.

Five days after he disappeared and two days after William Sandeson was arrested, the Sigma Chi international fraternity issued a statement on its website:

Our collective hearts and prayers are with Samson's chapter brothers and the family and friends who survive him. We also send our sincere appreciation to the Halifax Regional Police for their tireless and expedient work in helping to bring clarity to an otherwise senseless tragedy. Our priority is to assist, in whatever capacity we can, in the long healing process which will now take place for those who will struggle with the reality of this tragedy. In the meantime, we ask for privacy and patience in the days and weeks ahead.

But the frat brothers have been largely absent ever since. They did not testify at the trial, nor did they attend.

Lowe says it's because the brothers didn't know anything about the narrative that unfolded. Taylor's mother isn't so sure about that.

"They know more than what they've ever said," she says in the summer of 2017.

One of Taylor's frat brothers, who did not respond to a request to be interviewed for this book, posted a link to a news article during the trial showing a picture of Sandeson. "Rot, you son of a bitch," he wrote.

Lowe says Taylor loved being a member of the frat and really believed in the organization.

"He loved every single one of his brothers and he always wanted to make everyone be the best that they could be. He loved bringing people together. He never wanted anyone to feel excluded. He literally went the extra mile to make sure people were trying to get along and having a good time. It was the perfect environment for him, because he was such a leader organically like that."

His friends also say he was a natural entrepreneur, and constantly searched for ways to make money. One might assume Taylor planned to achieve this plan by selling drugs, but his family and friends insist he was also looking for other, legitimate, ways to make money.

He joined Vemma, a multi-level marketing business, started a YouTube tutoring business, a smoothie business, and had just started to think about getting into real estate.

"I think that that desire, and almost the need, to want to make a better life, because he wasn't satisfied with what he was seeing and what he had in life. Or it didn't match up with what he wanted or he felt like people around him deserved. I think that's really the most important part, is that he felt others deserved more," says Lowe.

Virtually everyone in Taylor's life knew he was selling drugs. They all say he talked about getting out of it.

"Oh my God, there's so many times we talked about that," says McCrossin. "I did his taxes every year and every year I'd say, 'Taylor, we're saying zero here. Obviously this isn't going to go on for the rest of your life.'" Taylor would always agree, yet he continued dealing.

His friends and family all agree he had no idea what he was getting into the night he died, and furthermore that he had never done anything like it before.

TAYLOR SAMSON IS MISSING

Taylor Samson was last seen on Saturday, August 15, but it was two nights earlier that the suspicious circumstances surrounding his death really began. In May 2017, his girlfriend of six months testified in court that a group of people were sitting around the common room at Taylor's apartment on Thursday evening when a person named "Devon" showed up with a black bag. Mackenzie Ruthven testified she had never seen the guy before, that Taylor immediately took him upstairs to his bedroom, and when they came back down they did not have the black bag. Ruthven told the jury Devon stayed only a short time and Taylor made an awkward introduction.

"Devon reached across the table to introduce himself, and paused with, "My name is—" and Taylor filled in with "Devon," she explained.

She described him as tall and socially awkward with short brown hair and a dark face that looked rough, with unkempt eyebrows. "He was just really awkward," she continued.

She didn't see Taylor too much throughout the day on August 15 because he had baseball and went to the gym. She had woken up early and gone back to her own apartment because an exchange student she was hosting from Italy wanted to ride the Harbour Hopper and go to Peggys Cove. They were planning a night out together with friends that night.

Taylor wanted to give the exchange student a taste of downtown Halifax, and was rounding up a group of friends to go to Pacifico, a local nightclub, but Ruthven said he seemed antsy and disengaged.

"I don't know how to label it," she told the jury. "He didn't seem particularly focused on going out. He seemed a little bit distracted."

Taylor was in the process of moving into a new apartment in the back of his frat house, and that's where he was with his girlfriend that night, before leaving just before 10:30 P.M.

"He said he was just going a couple houses down and would be right back," Ruthven testified, telling the jury he left his keys, his wallet, and his medication on the living-room table and took only his cellphone and a black bag with him. She believed it was the same black bag "Devon" had arrived with two nights prior, but couldn't be sure. She believed the bag contained a fair amount of marijuana, roughly four pounds.

She knew Taylor was involved in the drug trade and had seen him use drugs, but didn't really know much about his dealing. "He tried very hard to hide it from me," she testified, so that night she had no reason to believe he wouldn't be back in a few minutes as he had promised.

Meanwhile, Taylor's brother, Connor, was already out at a bar with friends in Amherst, a somewhat unusual activity for the more shy, withdrawn brother. Just before 10:30, their mother got a strange feeling, mother's intuition, perhaps.

"Something in my gut told me I better call Connor. Don't ask me why I never thought of Taylor," she says during our interview. "I figured Taylor was fine; it was Connor, because Connor never normally went out, and I thought, *he's out with friends, they're drinking, they're going to a bar, something's wrong.*"

When Connor didn't answer several calls, his mother sent a Facebook message. It was 10:27 P.M., one minute after Taylor walked into Sandeson's apartment. "Answer the fucking phone," was all it took, before Connor called her back to let her know he was fine. Linda Boutilier was right to be worried, but she was worried about the wrong son.

When Taylor didn't return, his girlfriend and his friends waited at his apartment a while and then proceeded downtown. Ruthven began calling and texting around 12:30 A.M., but the phone just rang and rang before eventually going to voicemail. She called again around 2:45. This time the phone went straight to voicemail, leading her to believe it was either off or the battery had died.

The next day, Taylor, who had even played baseball with a broken hand, didn't show up for a game. That's when his friend Shayn Power decided the matter was serious enough to pay Taylor's father a visit.

Dean Samson says he "worked at everything" until he suffered a stroke. He was a crew member at Dalhousie University's Rebecca Cohn Auditorium and at Halifax's Neptune Theatre, did stints as a photographer, and spent a few months as a reporter for a community newspaper. Later in life he did carpentry work. He started a degree in English at Saint Mary's University but never finished.

Samson's stepmother, Karen Burke, went back to high school when she was forty-one so that she could go on to take the LPN course. Her husband had left and she had to find a way to support her own children. She's currently off on disability after breaking a hand. The injury led to something called complex regional pain syndrome, a little-understood form of chronic pain that usually affects an arm or leg and typically develops after an injury.

Burke recalls that moment in August 2015 when Taylor's friend showed up with the news.

"He came in the door and he looked like something's up and he goes, 'Taylor's missing,' she says in an interview in the Halifax apartment to which she and Taylor's father had recently moved in the summer of 2017.

He did not provide the details of what Taylor had been doing the night before. Burke worried he had become ill after drinking alcohol, due to his liver condition, and decided to call around to see if he was at any of the area hospitals. He wasn't there. Still, Burke thought he might be unconscious, so she called back again asking if there was anyone at the hospitals whose identity was unknown. That wasn't the case either.

"No, there's something really serious here, Karen," said Taylor's friend, trying to explain the gravity of the situation, suggesting she should call the police.

"So I called the police," she says.

Officers first asked her if Taylor had suicidal tendencies. When she explained that he did not, they wanted to know if he had any medical conditions. She told them about the liver condition. "That's how it all started," she recalls thoughtfully, before continuing that her next move was to inform Taylor's mother. Burke says she tried to call, but there was no answer. It was now early evening on Sunday, and Taylor's mother and brother were at the grocery store, near their home in Amherst. Taylor was supposed to be coming home for a visit that day, but they weren't sure what time.

"We were just walking, and I was thinking, I *wonder if Taylor's in town yet. He's got to be in town by now.* So I messaged him and I didn't get an answer, so I called him and it went right to voicemail." She thought that must mean he was still driving and unable to answer his phone.

A few minutes later, at 6:01 P.M., Connor got a Facebook message from his father: "connor, taylor has been missing since last night, we don't know where he is, not in the E.R. or jail...we want your mom to know. love you xoxo"

There was no response before another message came in: "tell your mom to call us ASAP."

When there was no response again, the message got more frantic: *"IF YOU HAVE A PHONE SEND ME THE #"*

That's when Connor finally saw the messages.

"I was kind of panicked, just like 'Mom, mom, mom!'" he explains two years later.

"What?" his mother responded.

"Taylor's gone missing," he continued.

"What do you mean, 'Taylor's gone missing'?" his mother questioned, trying to comprehend what her younger son was telling her.

He showed her the message from his father. "She gave like that blank stare," says Connor.

"My whole body just went into a tremble," says Linda. "I've never experienced anything like it before in my life."

By this time, they weren't that far from home, but they ran the rest of the way and called Taylor's father and stepmother to find out what they knew. Then they packed up and drove to Halifax to meet up with Taylor's friends. They all clearly recall the moment they learned Taylor was missing—what they were doing and what they did next.

Kaitlynne Lowe was in Vancouver for a conference when she got a text from a friend on Sunday morning.

"Something's going on," it said. "Don't worry yet, gonna let you know when I know more."

He called her a couple of hours later.

"I was standing near Stanley Park in Vancouver, and he was telling me essentially not to freak out, that something bad had happened. I had thought that like my cat had got out or something and that's what he was telling me, and then he's just like, 'It's Taylor.'"

"Where is he? Who was he meeting? What happened?" Lowe shot back, but no one had those answers and that's what was most concerning to her.

"I don't really know too much about Taylor's dealing. I saw some of it, and I knew about it, but it was never anything that he went into specifically, but what I knew and what I trusted was that they would all know, anyone that was involved with Taylor would know. I didn't expect it to be that much of a secret."

She tried desperately to get an earlier flight home, but couldn't as she was already scheduled to leave the next morning.

By then word of Taylor's disappearance was rapidly spreading on social media. That's where Ryan Wilson got the news.

"When I first heard about it, I was like, 'Why is this such a big deal? Why is this all over Facebook? He's been gone for not even a day.'"

Wilson says he saw no reason to be worried. He recalled other occasions when he and Taylor had been out having a good time and not come home, and he believed Taylor would not get himself into a situation that would have repercussions. It wasn't until he found out where Taylor was going that night that he knew the situation was serious.

Thomas McCrossin got text messages directly from Linda and Connor but, thinking they were just messaging him some tax questions as he was also their accountant, he didn't look at the messages until Sunday evening. At that point Linda and Connor were already in Halifax, searching for Taylor. "We went banging on doors and I'm looking around, seeing if I can see Taylor's shoes," she says. They did that until one o'clock in the morning. She even unknowingly knocked on William Sandeson's door, but she recalls there were no lights on.

It wasn't until the next morning that Taylor's friends told his mother what he was up to the night before. Thomas McCrossin says he was walking up to Taylor's apartment when Linda came running down the street screaming his name and crying, "He's fucking dead!"

He was confused. "What? What's going on?"

"He had four pounds on him and they didn't tell me until now. They killed him," she told McCrossin.

Taylor's other friends, who had tried to protect him, at first believing the drugs would get him in trouble, had genuinely believed Taylor had been trying to sell four pounds of marijuana the night he disappeared.

McCrossin, who had no knowledge of Taylor's Saturday night plans, responded, "We're going to the fucking police station right now."

Sergeant Tanya Chambers-Spriggs testified at the trial that she was told Boutilier was at the front door of police headquarters with a friend of her son's on the morning of Monday, August 17, 2015, and was quite upset. Chambers-Spriggs told the jury she and another officer went to speak with Boutilier and McCrossin.

"There was nothing that initially stood out about his missing person report," she said in court. "When Ms. Boutilier came in she was quite distraught."

Chambers-Spriggs said that's when Boutilier disclosed that her son had an autoimmune liver disease and could die within three to five days of not having his medication. She also disclosed that Taylor's friends had told her that he may have had four pounds of marijuana on him. That information kicked the case up to the Major Crime Unit.

Boutilier says one of the officers told her, "I've been on the force for over thirty years, I'm telling you nobody dies over marijuana."

She responded, "And I'm telling you, something happened to Taylor."

It was the next day when officers told her she was right.

Boutilier was outside Taylor's apartment having a cigarette when Connor and McCrossin returned home from picking up a friend at the train station when two officers came walking up the driveway. Boutilier says she knew something was wrong, so she sent the boys inside.

"He said, 'Come on, let's go talk,'" she says, and then she starts to cry. "I knew."

"Let's go get a coffee," the officer said, but Boutilier refused.

"Where is he?" she demanded.

"We don't know," said the officer, and Boutilier repeated evenly, "Where is Taylor?"

"We don't know," the officer said again, as he walked toward her with the words that would change her world.

"Linda, with the evidence we have collected, we think Taylor may have met with foul play."

Boutilier took off running, down the street, through the alley-way, towards the Asian grocery store by William Sandeson's apartment. "Don't ask me why," she says. "I went up the step, trying to grab the door at Will's place, trying to get in."

She knew the police had already been there, but thought they were just looking for fingerprints to show that Taylor had been in that apartment. "Nothing else ever crossed my mind," she says.

Next came the impossible task of informing her son and Taylor's friends that their worst fears had been realized.

"Linda just sort of barged," recalls McCrossin. "'I need you, you, you, you.'" Boutilier pointed at Taylor's closest friends. "'Everyone else, go!'"

Then she pulled McCrossin up the stairs inside Taylor's apartment. "I need you to sit by Connor right now," she told him. "They're charging somebody with first-degree murder."

The scene that was about to unfold would be dramatic.

"When Thomas held my hand and said it was going to be okay, it was that feeling that no, it's not," says Connor, describing the moment before police told the small group they were charging someone with first-degree murder in the death of his brother. Connor says he was in shock at first and then he "freaked bad."

"I'm sitting there, and Connor's just hyperventilating," says McCrossin. "I'm just sitting there, like *what the hell do I do?* I'm like, 'I love you buddy' and he's like, 'Fuck off! It doesn't matter.'"

By then Linda had gone outside to speak further with the officers.

"I heard Connor in there just bawling and screaming," she says. "They had him, one on each side of him, trying to bring him down the steps. He could barely walk."

They took Connor to the hospital emergency department where doctors tried to explain how his autism would affect the feelings he was experiencing and gave him some medication to help him relax. Connor immediately believed his brother was dead, but his mother did not.

"I didn't feel it," she says, two years later, "I still don't." For Boutilier it was just the beginning of a never-ending search for her son's body, without which she could not, would not, achieve the closure she sought.

CHAPTER 4

WHO IS WILLIAM SANDESON?

William Sandeson was born on September 27, 1992, the first child of Laurie and Michael Sandeson. They would go on to have three more sons and raise them on a small farm, where Michael also grew up, in Lower Truro, about one hundred kilometres outside of Nova Scotia's capital.

The farm was largely cattle, although the family also sold hay, consisting of approximately 150 acres in one lot, with the back half, or woodlot, mostly owned by William's paternal grandmother, plus 60 to 70 acres of grassland in various spots. The Sandesons bought it from Michael's parents.

By all accounts, William and his brothers had a normal, happy childhood, with dedicated parents who took them on family trips to Florida and the Dominican Republic. Raised in a middle-class family, William also had the opportunity to visit Italy and Greece on a school trip and travelled around Europe a little more while visiting a friend in Ireland.

Besides operating the farm at home, their father had a part-time job driving a delivery truck, delivering bags of feed. His mother had worked as a civil servant in the provincial Department of Agriculture for twenty-seven years as of 2015. She was the coordinator of a 4-H program as well as the department's innovation coordinator.

Eugene Tan, who would become William's defence lawyer, was also his volleyball coach, through which he became a Sandeson family friend.

"Honestly, I don't think you could find a nicer family," says Tan during an interview in his Halifax office following Sandeson's trial. "They're incredibly devoted to their kids."

Tan says all four Sandeson boys are very active and their parents always attend their events. They're also attractive. William, with dirty-blond hair, blue eyes, a closely trimmed beard, and a lean build, is boyishly good-looking, the epitome of clean-cut.

Tan first met him in 2009 or 2010 at a time when coaching volleyball was a significant hobby of his. Will was attending high school at the Cobequid Educational Centre in Truro, but Tan's Halifax team was attracting players from outside the city and Will was good enough to be one of them. Tan says, despite not being overly tall, at five foot ten, Sandeson was incredibly athletic and a tenacious player. According to their parents, William's brothers, Adam, who was twenty when his oldest brother was arrested, Matthew, sixteen, and David, fourteen, were very close. David was once asked to write about his hero for a school project and chose to write about William. His brothers looked up to him, and why wouldn't they?

"He never gives up on anything, he just never ever stops moving," says Tan. "In any sport, you'll see plays where people will kind of give up, and most of the time, rightfully, you know they'll see that this ball is just completely unplayable, they're not going to get it. He's the guy who's gonna jump over the first row of chairs through the stands to try and play that ball. That's the kind of player he was."

That said, Tan admits he didn't know Will overly well as a player, having only coached him for about a year, but got to know him better when Will moved to Halifax to attend Dalhousie University in 2010. Tan was then the assistant coach for the Dalhousie men's volleyball team. Will tried out for that team, but didn't make it. Instead, he was hired as the team statistician, a role he held for four and a half years.

Tan got to know the family better while coaching Will's younger brother, Adam, on the Canada Games Team in 2013. At that level, he was doing three-hour sessions four to five times a week and says he saw Mike and Laurie Sandeson at least two or three times a week. He says the parents' devotion to their four boys cannot be overstated.

"They've all done well, they've all done well in school, they're incredibly kind, incredibly generous people," Tan says.

Cellphone reports obtained by the author following Sandeson's trial show text exchanges between Will and his parents that reflect the normal loving upbringing Tan describes.

"We plan to watch Dal Tigers play MUN tomorrow evening," his mom texted one day after Will had moved away to university. "Do you want us to bring anything along?"

"Hamburger soup is great thanks," Will responded.

The report is riddled with typical messages a mother might send a son.

"Dr. Johnston's office is desperately trying to get you back in to fit your retainer. Please call their office and set up a time!"

"You forgot to take your pie." And "You left some of your clothes hanging on the drying rack."

"Just found the bunny, thank you and happy Easter!" William texted his mom in April 2015. "And the same to you. We still want to get down to take you and Adam out for a celebration meal," his mom replied.

"Are you home safe and sound?" she asked in June 2015.

"Home safe!" Will replied.

"Thanks I can go to sleep now. Hope you have a good sleep. Love mom."

A record of messages with his father also illustrates a typical father-son relationship.

"Heading to Cavendish in the early morning tomorrow. Stopping in to grab tent and sleeping bags on the way," William texted his dad.

"Tent and BBQ in wheelbarrow in basement. Probably won't be home when you get here," his dad responded.

"Coming to Hfx to fix Adam's door. Anything you want? Have truck," his dad asked another day.

THE PERFECT SON

William was everything any parent would be proud of. He had completed his undergrad, a bachelor of science with first-class honours in kinesiology, with aspirations of becoming a doctor, and while he didn't make the varsity volleyball team, he did make the track team, and would go on to run track for the Dalhousie Tigers right up until he was arrested.

In a statement to police, one of his teammates said he was "spoiled rotten," that he was never "around drugs and the rush of everything." Justin Blades, who would eventually play an important role in the case, also described Will as "soft," saying he "couldn't fucking beat his way out of a paper bag." Blades said Sandeson did have an angry side while he was drinking, a side of him he believed came from the fact he was "supressed at home growing up." He didn't offer any explanation as to exactly what that meant.

The Tigers track team has, over the years, been successful enough to count Olympians Geoff Harris (London 2012) and Adrienne Power (Beijing 2008) among its alumni. Sandeson's specialty was middle-distance running, and he was fast. An online athletic profile shows his personal bests at several events. In June 2013, he ran 400 metres in 50.81 seconds at a race in Moncton, New Brunswick. Two months later, in Sherbrooke, Quebec, he ran 800 metres in 1 minute 55.37 seconds. In February 2015, he competed in Boston, where he completed a 400-metre race in 50.50 seconds, and just five months before he was arrested, in March 2015, Sandeson headed back to Moncton where he ran 300 metres in 37.06 seconds.

Running track was a sport Sandeson shared with his girlfriend, Sonja Gashus, whom he had begun dating in January 2015. Gashus was gorgeous with long brown hair and long legs. A commerce major from Dartmouth, Nova Scotia, her speciality was sprinting.

The track team would end up being at the centre of the most shocking twist in the Sandeson trial—the twist that sparked calls for a mistrial.

It seemed that everything William Sandeson was doing was geared toward his interest in medicine, specifically sports medicine. While doing his undergrad at Dal, he went to Ghana on a medical brigade mission to help treat people in a small village.

After failing to get into Dal's med school on his first attempt, he went to Saba University's School of Medicine, a school located on Saba, a special municipality of the Netherlands in the Caribbean. That's where he got his passion permanently tattooed on his body—an emblem widely recognized as a medical symbol of two snakes wrapped around a staff.

It is not uncommon for Canadian students to attend medical schools in the Caribbean after being rejected at Canadian schools. It's also not uncommon for some to transfer back to a school like Dal after being accepted to the med school while studying at Saba, as was the case with William Sandeson, but the credits are not transferrable.

Saba is also not on the list of the Royal College of Physicians and Surgeons of Canada's approved jurisdictions, which means even if students complete medical degrees there, they still require further certification in order to practise medicine in Nova Scotia. But William Sandeson wouldn't have to worry about that.

After only five months on the Caribbean island, Sandeson returned to Halifax, where he began working as a personal trainer at Dal between December 2013 and September 2014, which is how he met Tanya Bilsbury. (He was also a personal trainer at GoodLife Fitness for a couple of months prior to heading to the Caribbean.)

"I remember him as laughing and charming; we had fun," says Bilsbury, who was also a student at Dal and now works for the federal government. "I really had fun in my personal training sessions with him."

In an interview, Bilsbury says he told her that he was working twelve-hour shifts in an effort to pay off debt he had wracked up going to school in the Caribbean. She says he was also paranoid she wasn't going to pay for her personal training sessions, which she thought was strange because she knew it was her responsibility to pay Dal, not his.

Sandeson quit his job as a personal trainer in September 2014 and began working for Regional Residential Services, a non-profit organization that runs group homes and small options homes for adults who live with disabilities. He worked at a house where three residents lived, two men and a woman, who were reliant on him for medication, food, personal care, even moving about the house, and certainly to leave the house to do errands.

At the same time, Sandeson also worked as a patient attendant in the emergency and trauma centre of the QEII Health Sciences Centre in Halifax, seemingly valuable experience while working toward that goal of becoming a doctor.

Tanya Bilsbury ran into him at the Dalplex in the summer of 2015 and he told her he had finally been accepted to Dal's medical school. The coveted positions require a grade point average of 3.3 for students from the Maritime provinces (3.7 for students from elsewhere in Canada) and a minimum score of 503 on the MCAT (Medical College Admission Test).

"I was so happy for him," she says. "I remember him running— he was so fast, he was like a streak—and I was watching him thinking, *wow he's really got everything he could want.*"

But eight days before his white-coat ceremony was to take place, William Sandeson set in motion a series of events that would ensure he would never become a doctor.

WILL SANDESON LINKED TO CASE

For Will Sandeson, August 15, 2015, started out as a day like any other. He woke up with his girlfriend who had spent the night; he went to work and she went to the market before heading to Rainbow Haven Beach outside Dartmouth, where she spent the day with a girlfriend. They both returned to Will's apartment around 5 P.M. and watched an episode of *Scandal,* an American political thriller series, on Netflix, before heading to Stubborn Goat, a downtown Halifax restaurant.

While they were eating dinner, William told Sonja he was going to have some people over that night and that she shouldn't be there, so she made plans to visit her friend, who lived a few houses away from Will's apartment, and they watched a movie, *The Fault in Our Stars.* She had to work early the next morning at Starbucks, so when the movie was over, she texted Will that she wanted to come home, and he said, "Okay, won't be too much longer," until he eventually told her to come home between midnight and 12:30.

Gashus told police that when she arrived back at Will's, the two-bedroom apartment reeked of bleach, and he told her he had poured it all over the floor to clean up. "And he said that the guys that were there, one guy just snapped and just, like, attacked the other guy and he bled everywhere," Gashus recounted.

She said she asked Will if the guy was okay, and he said, "Well, he, like, stumbled out." She told police she thought it was sketchy, but she had to work early so she went to bed.

Gashus said Will was pretty shaken up when she got home that night. "When we were in bed, like, I laid on his chest, and his was like, sweaty, and his heart was pounding."

The next morning, the couple woke up early and Will drove Sonja to work around 5:45, picking up her co-worker along the way. Will didn't have to be at work at the group home until 12:30.

"When he came in, he told us that he had gone out with his girlfriend for food the night before and he was really full still from that," testified his co-worker Frances Myketyn-Driscoll. "And he was coughing a bit and he said he had been cleaning and might be coughing more through the day 'cause he inhaled some bleach fumes," she went on, describing his demeanour as regular.

Myketyn-Driscoll said she and Sandeson took all three of the residents out to do errands at Walmart and the Superstore, and he drove the van, interacting with the residents normally. Later as Sandeson and a co-worker were doing laundry for the residents, it was discovered he was also doing some of his own, but that was not entirely out of the ordinary.

Meanwhile, Sonja saw posts that Taylor Samson was missing going around on Facebook, so she shared it with Will. "And I was like, 'This isn't the guy that got beat up, is it?'" she told police. "And he was like, 'Thank God, no. He was definitely not six four.'"

Sonja arrived back at Will's place around 10:30 Sunday evening and waited for him to get home from work, shortly after. The conversation that night wasn't great, as Sonja, who had been kind of mad at Will for a couple of days, was still pissed off, although she was also worried about him. She said he was on his phone a lot, and she told him, "You're just off." That night when they went to bed, Sonja asked Will, "Do you know what happened to that guy?" and he said, "No, just cut off all ties to everybody." He thought she would be happy because she knew he was a drug dealer—in fact he had done multiple deals in her presence and she had repeatedly asked him to stop—and he had told her this was the end; he was auctioning off all of his clients.

The next day, Monday, August 17, Frances Myketyn-Driscoll was back at work at the group home when two police officers showed up at the door just before midnight. Taylor Samson's phone was never found, but police obtained the last number contacted by his phone, from Iristel, the telecommunications provider. They traced the number to the group home in Lower Sackville.

Myketyn-Driscoll and a co-worker answered questions for roughly two hours and showed one officer the staff computer, from which officers believed the message to Taylor Samson had been sent. When the officers left, a worker named Felicia Butler texted Will Sandeson and another colleague who was on shift at the time the message went out, asking if they knew Taylor Samson. It was 12:41 in the morning on August 18.

"Will this is Felicia. Do you know Taylor Sampson? The cops just showed up saying the last known message to him was from here and now he is a missing person. They are going to contact you."

"Ok, thanks!" Will responded just before 8 A.M.

"No worries! Just thought I'd give you a heads up."

"Appreciated! I tried to get a hold of him when he wasn't answering anyone," Will replied.

"Oh okay," answered his co-worker.

The next day, Will's co-workers informed their supervisor about what had occurred. The supervisor, in turn, called the lead investigator at the time and informed her that the connection was Will Sandeson. The supervisor also called Will and left him a voicemail to let him know the investigator was looking to speak with him. He texted her back around 10:15 A.M. Tuesday morning to let her know he got the message.

The case was now connected to Sandeson, even if it wasn't exactly clear how.

CHAPTER 5
A VOLUNTARY WITNESS

A round 11:30 A.M. on August 18, RCMP Sergeant Charla Keddy was asked to try to get in touch with William Sandeson. At the time, she was told police had determined the last number to contact Taylor Samson had somehow been related to Sandeson, and they wanted Keddy and her colleague to speak with him about when he last saw or contacted Samson.

Keddy called the number she was provided, left a voice-mail and a text message, and Sandeson called her back shortly after and willingly agreed to meet with her within twenty to thirty minutes. He arrived at Halifax Police Headquarters on Gottingen Street, as promised, just before 1 P.M.

Keddy had been a police officer for just over fifteen years, starting out as a general-duty officer in Barrington, Nova Scotia, before transferring to the Halifax Federal Serious and Organized Crime Unit in 2007. In 2014, she was awarded the Atlantic Women in Law Enforcement Officer of the Year.

Sandeson was not a suspect or under any kind of suspicion during that first interview. When she testified, Keddy said he was polite and co-operative.

It seemed he believed he was in control of the situation, but he would make a critical mistake in that interview.

Keddy showed the video to the jury.

It takes place in a bright open room with a couch and an armchair, with the door unlocked. Sandeson is wearing a T-shirt and shorts with sneakers and a backwards baseball cap.

Unbeknownst to both parties, it's only hours before the real interrogation would begin following Sandeson's arrest. Keddy identifies herself as an RCMP sergeant on the homicide team.

Keddy asks Sandeson to tell her a bit about how he knows Samson and the last time he saw him.

"Last time I saw him was this Thursday past," Sandeson begins, already lying.

"Okay."

"And I met up with him...I really...I didn't even know his last name until I saw him on the news but I just think I met him three weeks ago...."

"Uh-huh."

"...through selling some cannabis."

"Okay. All right."

"I wanted to see what he had."

Sandeson tells the officer that he and Samson talked back and forth a little since they had met through a mutual friend. When he saw him on Thursday, he was checking out a sample. Two other guys were with Samson, and a girl Sandeson thought was his girlfriend. He tells Keddy he hasn't seen him since. It wasn't true.

"And then he didn't respond to a text on Saturday night. I texted him Saturday night. I texted him again Sunday." That wasn't true either.

"Okay, all right. So let's rewind for a bit. We're going to go back to the beginning. So you said you first met him three weeks ago approximately?"

"Uh-huh."

"Okay. So who introduced you to him?"

"This guy...I don't know his last name."

"That's all right."

"His first name's Jeff. I know where he lives."

"Okay."

"He's a Dal student."

"Yeah. So Jeff introduced you to him for what reasoning?"

"For me to buy marijuana."

Police were unable to confirm whether Jefferson Guest was in fact the one who introduced Samson and Sandeson, but they do believe it to be true. Guest did not respond to a request to participate in this book.

In the video, Sandeson tells Keddy the conversation between him and Samson was patchy because Samson travelled a bit, leaving town and coming back, and then again, until they finally met on that Thursday night.

"He told me where to meet. We met on Robie Street."

"Uh-huh."

"He couldn't get into where he wanted to get into and his girlfriend was with him—I assume, I think it was his girlfriend. Anyway, he couldn't get in and then we went to another apartment off Henry Street, close to my place...where all the police are right now."

"Okay. So where was the place that he tried to get into that he couldn't get into Thursday night?" Keddy asks.

"It was really close on Robie Street. I can go back and find out," Sandeson says.

"Is it in your messages or whatever, phone messages?"

"Yeah."

"Okay. You can scroll through if you want. If you think it's in your phone."

"As...as soon as he went missing...I had a texting app and I deleted the texting app."

"Okay. And why did you delete it?"

"I got nervous about selling marijuana."

On the Thursday night, Sandeson says, he and Samson ended up at another apartment close to his place on Henry Street. Keddy wants to know who was there when they went inside.

"There were two guys upstairs in a door[way]. There's a guy sitting on the couch here, on the couch there."

"Did you know any of the people that were there?"

"I didn't know anyone there, no."

"All right. And so what happened when you were in the apartment?"

"He went upstairs to the right and came down with a duffle bag and just opened it up and basically showed what he had."

"Okay. And how much marijuana do you think was in the duffle bag that he showed you?"

"There were two big...what's it called...vacuum-sealed bags. Probably was two pounds at one point but it looked like they'd been dug into a bit."

Sandeson says he didn't take any that night because the quality wasn't very good.

"I mean, the introduction was to meet someone with something really nice, and that wasn't, so I just didn't take anything," he says.

He says Samson was disappointed that he didn't want the weed and was going to look for something better.

"After that...I don't know if we talked Friday at all. I worked Friday, Saturday, Sunday, yesterday, out in Sackville. I don't think I heard from him Friday, I didn't hear anything, and then Saturday he was anxious to meet me but I was at work pretty much all day."

"Uh-huh."

"And then after work, I went out for dinner with my girlfriend and—"

"Where did you go to dinner at?"

"The Stubborn Goat."

Sandeson tells the officer he had some drinks at the restaurant and then went home and had a few more. His girlfriend went to a friend's apartment across the street to watch a movie and he went to hang out with his neighbour.

It's here that William Sandeson begins to seriously lie to Sergeant Keddy.

"And [Samson] had been texting, wanting to show me the new thing that he had got."

"Uh-huh."

"And I said, 'Okay, I'll take a look' and then...it was bad communication because I was drinking and I didn't...and my phone's always on silent, so I didn't check back and forth."

He starts to ramble.

"I think I missed a call from him and then I called him back and he said he had to run somewhere for a while and then would be back. So I think we decided...we had a time set. At some point there was a time, and then that time passed. I texted him wondering where he was, no answer, and then I texted him the next morning too... wondering and then a friend...Jeff told me that he was missing."

Keddy asks him to go back over his Saturday a little more. He says he left the Stubborn Goat around nine.

"So during this whole time, is Taylor still messaging you or are you messaging back and forth while you're having supper?"

"I didn't have my phone out so—"

"Okay. Oh wow."

"I was trying not to do it. I did today at lunch and I got grilled for it so I figured...No, I don't think I even got a message waiting because I said I couldn't meet until a lot later that night."

He was supposed to meet Samson around 10 or 10:30, after his girlfriend, Sonja, left, he says. When she did leave, he continued drinking by himself, watching Netflix, and cleaning, and then when Samson said he'd be a while longer, Sandeson went to his neighbour's to see if he had anything to smoke. Pookiel McCabe didn't have any drugs.

"So I just had another beer and then went back to my apartment and then I saw...I think I saw a missed call from him, so I called him back again. He said, 'Oh, you missed your window' or whatever.

'Now if you want any, I have to go get more.'"

"Uh-huh."

"And I went, 'Okay, yeah, like I'll wait. Go get more.' And then I waited around. He didn't come...still didn't come. Then my girl-friend came back and then...well you can't...you can't come now. I think around 12 she got back, 12, 12:30. 'Well I can't take it now but if you can get some tomorrow, I'll still take it.'"

"So is that a message you sent him?"

"Yeah." Another lie.

"At around what time?"

"I think it was like 1:30. I was awake still."

"Okay."

"And then the next day I messaged wondering if he could bring it and then no response and then we found out he's missing."

Keddy wants to know what Sandeson knew about Samson.

"So little. I know that Jeff was good friends. He'd been dealing with him for a long time. He was into network marketing is what I understood because he said Jeff is starting a T-shirt company. So I thought he'd be a good friend to have because my roommate Pookiel is starting a T-shirt company."

[Pookiel McCabe actually lived across the hall from Sandeson in another apartment.]

"Yeah. And what kind of quantity were you looking at buying from him?"

"I just wanted a few grams for myself." It is the lie that would lead to Sandeson's demise.

"Uh-huh."

"But I know people who are looking for pounds, so I was curious if he had a good price on something then I could just put people in contact with each other."

"Okay. Did you ever put him in contact with any of those people that you knew?"

"No."

"Did you ever share his information...his phone number or

anything with anyone to get...to call him?" It's a question that indicates police do not yet suspect William Sandeson of anything other than buying and selling marijuana to which he freely admitted.

"No, no, I didn't share it."

Sandeson explains his own phone number. He had a texting application, called Nextplus, on his phone that only works with Wi-Fi, and uses a number with an out-of-province area code. This is also where he tells Keddy he's a student at Dal.

"Okay. So what are you taking at Dal?" she asks.

"Medicine."

"Oh, are you?"

"Starting on Sunday."

He tells her he's from Lower Truro, just outside Truro, and that he's been in Halifax on and off for five years, willingly sharing the information. "I did my bachelor's in three years at Dal and then finished up. Worked a weird summer between Sackville-Truro, not Halifax. 2013 summer I lived...you probably don't need this much detail."

"No, that's okay."

"Anyway, sorry...I worked at GoodLife. I got hired at Truro GoodLife. I got trained in Sackville GoodLife."

"Uh-huh."

"Then I got accepted to medical school in the Caribbean, so I had to quit my job basically right when I finished training and went to school there—"

"Where at?"

"...the end of August. Saba."

"Okay."

"It's a very, very small island."

"Where is it near? Is it near St. Kitts and all that?"

"Yeah. St. Maarten...I fly into St. Maarten...and from there either...it's the smallest commercial airway in the world so...you either take a twenty-person plane over or an hour-and-a-half ferry."

"Yeah, okay."

"And did a semester there. Hated it, on the island. Came back here. Worked in Halifax now, I came back Christmas 2013 to a job at the Dalplex because I had worked there before. Then I worked at the Dalplex until I couldn't stand it anymore that summer and I got a job working in Sackville that I've had ever since."

"And this will be your first year of medical school here—"

"At Dal."

"Did your stuff in the Caribbean count towards credits?"

"No. Kind of soars my debt."

Trying to establish Sandeson's motive for killing Taylor Samson, the Crown would raise his debt issue during the trial, bringing in records showing Sandeson had run up his line of credit to $78,000.

"Okay. Yeah, I'm sure," says Keddy. "So now that you're here...so you have your motorbike. Do you have any other vehicles?"

Sandeson tells Keddy he had two other vehicles—a truck for the farm that stayed in Truro and a Mazda Protegé, for which he had an appointment to get the brakes fixed that afternoon.

"Okay. And how long have you been kind of in the marijuana scene for, do you figure?"

"Two...I knew people before I left for the Caribbean but I hadn't like made any money off of it."

"Yeah, okay."

"And I hadn't smoked anything until January, last year, was the first time I tried it."

"Uh-huh."

"And then from January, I just met a few people because I was always interested in trying new things. And then after meeting some people I just found out that you basically just sell a phone number for a few hundred dollars."

The officer tells Sandeson she is going to take a break and he can just think while she's gone, but he continues talking.

"I don't know if Jeff's been in, but Jeff was asking me about seeing Taylor...and I was like well, 'where do you think he was trying to get weed from that night?' and he said he's never known who

Taylor got weed from, protecting his profit, wouldn't tell anyone but he said he seemed to think it was Sackville, and all he said was that the guys were deep or pretty serious, I think was the quote 'and they're pretty serious.'"

"And when do you first find out about Taylor missing?"

"Saturday."

Taylor wasn't missing on Saturday.

"Saturday?" the officer questions.

"Or...the...the day after. So I had three unresponded to texts the next, that day when I was at work. So Sunday."

These are the texts he sent as part of his cover up.

"And who told you that he was missing?"

"Someone...someone else who sells."

"Okay. And who was that?"

"His name's Jordan. I don't know his last name, but I also know where he lives. He said that he was missing, or do you know where Taylor is and I said, 'No, why? And Taylor who?'"

The young man would later be revealed to be Jordan MacEwan, and he would tell a story of his own.

Sandeson tells Keddy that MacEwan told him Taylor was supposed to drop off some money the night before, $900, but he didn't show up.

"And I said, 'Well, I was supposed to see him too and he didn't come around.' But that was it and I didn't know if they knew each other until that day."

A BIG MISTAKE

Keddy leaves the room and comes back ten minutes later. By now William Sandeson has been in the interview room for nearly forty minutes. He seems to believe he has totally outsmarted the police.

"I just have a couple other questions for you, Will, and then we'll finish up."

Keddy wants to know more about Sandeson's texting app.

"Okay. So when did you just delete the app?"

"Yesterday."

"Okay. And how come you deleted it yesterday and not earlier?"

"Because [Jordan] told me, he said, 'The police have his phone. I'm worried...do you think we'll get in trouble?'"

"Okay. And meaning, *will we get in trouble over what?*"

"For weed. Selling it."

"Okay."

"I'm like, 'Well, I haven't even thought of that. I don't think. I think they're just trying to find him.' And he said, 'Well, I'm probably going to ditch my phone,' and 'okay, well I think I'll delete the app then.'"

"And after you delete that app, you can't recover it and get all your contacts or no?"

"I'm not sure. I haven't tried."

Perhaps he should have tried because it was the recovery of that app that would allow police to begin to unravel his web of lies, an unusual mistake for someone of his apparent intelligence and of a generation typically very tech savvy.

Keddy continues questioning Sandeson about who was around when Taylor initially showed him the weed on Thursday, what they looked like, and who was aware of his drug involvement.

"And you said you have a girlfriend, right?"

"Uh-huh."

"Is she aware of your weed involvement?"

"Yes. She knows that if I ever needed any I had no problem finding it."

"And did she ever put you in touch with people or—"

"No, actually she's completely dead set against it, hates to hear about it, so that's why I was waiting for her to be gone."

It was not at all why he was waiting for his girlfriend to be gone. In fact she would later testify that she had seen him sell weed many times.

"Okay. Were you aware if Taylor...is he into any other drugs besides marijuana that you know about?"

"I know he bought mushrooms from Jordan."

"Okay. And have you ever had any other involvement with any other type of drug except for marijuana?"

"Last summer, a year ago, I had a couple of grams of MDMA that I bought personally."

"Okay. So just so that I have a clear picture, because it's important for us, when we do these types of investigations, for us to have a real good clear picture of everything and how it happened and who knew who and that kind of thing."

"Uh-huh."

"I just want to make sure that you're being completely honest about the marijuana part because that's not what we're investigating."

"Yeah."

"So if you were to sit here and tell me that you were buying pounds at a time and you were selling pounds at a time...you're not going to get in trouble for that."

"I never did through Taylor. I have, but I'd never done it through Taylor."

He explains that he had another person that he usually purchased from but had been shopping around for a new supplier.

"Would you ever pick it up and deliver it to each person?"

"I have."

"What kind of level would you be kind of almost like setting up for, kind of the middle man for?"

"I've never had more than a pound, but people have asked me for more, so then that's why, like never more than like ten was pretty typical. But it would be like 'Can you find ten?' and I'd put them in touch with the person that I normally just buy one from and then they get ten."

"Okay. So when he brings down his stuff to show you on Thursday when you're at the apartment, he's showing you because he knows that you're dealing potentially in pounds of marijuana."

"He knows, yeah."

"Okay. So initially when you were looking to meet up with him Saturday night, how much were you supposed to pick up from him?"

"I just wanted something for myself that night."

"Okay."

"Because I'd been drinking."

"Oh, okay. But you had been in touch with him earlier during the day right, while you were at work, when you weren't drinking, and you were supposed to meet him later that night."

"Yeah."

"So what was that for?"

"That was a sample on a large amount again that he wanted to show me."

"All right. So how much a large amount? How much did he want to sell you did he say that he had?"

"Twenty pounds."

"Okay, so he wanted to sell you twenty pounds?"

Sandeson nods. "And I couldn't take it. I didn't have anyone interested in it because, I assumed it was what he'd showed me before and I said, 'No, I can't, like I don't have anyone interested in that.'"

"Yeah, but he still wanted to meet you to give you a sample, right?"

"He still wanted to give me a sample and then as I started drinking, 'Well, sure I'll take a sample.'"

"Uh-huh. Okay. And then when you wrote back and you said, 'I can't meet you now because my girlfriend is back' or whatever, 'But I'll meet you to get it tomorrow from you.' So how much were you supposed to get from him the next day?"

"The sample."

"Just the sample?"

"I hadn't seen it yet so I couldn't verify that I could, I wasn't going to get it and hold onto it, and basically it was supposed to be like the end because I started school on Sunday."

"You were going to stop this."

"Not doing it anymore, and when I was drunk that night I texted my girlfriend, 'Good news, I'm all done.'"

THE DELETED TEXTS

Keddy asks Sandeson to tell her the story backwards. He does with ease. She then steps out and asks him to try to recover the texting app he deleted.

"If I just hop on any Wi-Fi—" he starts.

"Yeah, so maybe you might have to do it like when you're home or whatever to see if you can bring it back up," Keddy interjects.

"Or if there's wireless here, I could do it right now," Sandeson offers helpfully, seemingly unaware the app would restore all of his text history. Keddy eventually brings in someone to help Sandeson establish a personal hotspot. While they wait, she continues questioning.

"How much was Taylor looking for, pricewise, for what he had that you saw Thursday night?"

"Two thousand each."

Sandeson tells Keddy that when he met Samson on Thursday night, he had only two pounds on him, and he was asking different prices for each because they were two different types.

"Do you know what he was calling them? You know how some people call them grapefruit or kush or—?"

"I don't know what the expensive one was because it was already outside my price range and the other one was one of the gun ones, like AK-47 or 19 or something like that."

He says the most he'd ever had in his hands before was one pound, and the most he'd ever "middle-manned" for was five or ten pounds, for a guy who never ended up paying him.

"So how much were you out on that one?"

"Five thousand dollars. It was stupid. He paid me for part of it and then just never showed up again."

"So what do you think happened to Taylor? Have you heard anything?"

"In talking to people it just seemed...I don't think he...just, I don't know, left. Like, he said he had it, so if he left with it or if he sold it to someone else...and then I don't really know. I haven't heard from him so I assume he's hiding...but I don't really know."

There's a knock at the door. It's the tech officers asking questions about Sandeson's efforts to connect to the internet. They're trying to figure out a way to access the texting app he keeps referring to but says he's deleted.

They leave the room together, hoping the connection is better. Six minutes later they return, with Keddy explaining on the recording that they were able to recover the Nextplus texting app and the tech guys are going to take some screenshots of his messages from that night.

Sandeson helpfully searches his phone for the numbers of the contacts he and the officer had been discussing previously, and she asks to look at his conversations with Samson. He hands over the phone, pointing out that the app shows the times on the side of the conversation.

"He says at 10:24 P.M., 'I'm out back of the building now. Is that your bike parked by the door?' and you said, 'I'm walking out now.' So what happened then?" asks Keddy.

"I went out and there was no one there."

Not true.

"Okay."

"That's when I went over to Pookie's, and I guess he's not coming."

"Okay. And then you said, 'This isn't cool, man. You said you'd be right back.' So what happened in between the time you walked out and the time you sent the message, 'This isn't cool, man. You said you'd be right back.'?"

"I think I talked to him on the phone. There should be a phone—"

"Is that incoming at 10:24? Yeah, incoming. So he called you at 10:24?"

"Right."

"So at 10:24 he says, 'I'm out back of the building now. Is that your bike parked by the door?' You say, 'I'm walking out now' at 10:25. But he must have called you because there's an incoming call at 10:24."

"Yeah."

"What was that call about?"

"I think that was him saying, 'Too late.'"

"Even though you messaged back like one minute—"

"Yeah, one minute," Sandeson interrupts. "If you just scroll down to get more of the conversation. He was in like a weird hurry."

Keddy is holding strong, questioning all the odd things that don't add up in Sandeson's story, but what she doesn't know yet is that Sandeson's own video camera shows him leaving his apartment and coming back with Taylor Samson at 10:26. He believed his system recorded over itself every twenty minutes, which was another mistake with technology that Sandeson simply could not afford.

There's another knock on the door and Detective Constable Marshall Hewitt enters the room to photograph the phone. When that's complete, Keddy tells Sandeson she knows he has to get going to his car appointment. He offers to call to let them know he's running late, but Keddy says she'll drive him. Before they leave she wants to clarify one point—what happened when Sandeson told Samson he was on his way out of his building? Again, Sandeson tells her Samson wasn't there.

"And what about phone calls during that time?" asks Keddy.

"I called Taylor when I had a missed call from him at 11, I think."

"Uh-huh. Because on your phone it says that there is a missed call at 10:24."

"Yeah."

"So what was that?"

"That was him calling me."

"Okay, to say?"

"I think that might have been the call that I missed. Yeah, because that's the only one. I don't remember speaking to him on a call he made to me. I made calls to him."

"And that's when he said, 'You're too late' or whatever?"

"Yeah."

"Okay. Is there anything else you feel that's important for us to know?"

"No."

"If you do remember anything, you have my cellphone to call me, and if you hear anything as well, I'd want you to call us."

"I have asked quite a few people to look around, so if I do, yeah, absolutely, if I hear anything."

They begin to leave together, with Keddy planning to drive him to his appointment, when Sandeson backtracks into the room, glancing at the cameras and smiling, before telling Keddy he plans to go camping with his girlfriend the next day.

"What time are you leaving at?"

"She's working a half-day and has the afternoon off. She works at Investors Group in Dartmouth right now. So I'm picking her up from there and we're going to Keji [Kejimkujik National Park] and we're spending two nights, Wednesday, Thursday, back Friday, maybe, not sure any plans for like...it's kind of roughing it."

"Okay."

"But this Saturday I have to be back in Halifax. There's registration at the Med Campus at noon on Saturday."

But William Sandeson would never make it to med school registration. By noon on Saturday, he would be behind bars; in fact, he would be there before the end of the night.

That Tuesday afternoon, just before 3 P.M., Sergeant Charla Keddy and another officer drove him home in an unmarked vehicle to his apartment on Henry Street, before returning to headquarters, where investigators were now pouring over the text messages they had photographed on Sandeson's phone and discovering they didn't quite match up with what he had told Keddy. The texts made it clear Sandeson was *not* expecting Taylor to show up with a sample to smoke himself that Saturday night; he *was* expecting him to show up with twenty pounds of marijuana. The fact that he lied about it made him a suspect.

Several hours later, while he was at his girlfriend's grandmother's house in Dartmouth, William Sandeson was arrested. Sonja Gashus testified that as they were walking out the door after dinner, police officers who had been hovering around the driveway handcuffed them both. "I was confused and I asked questions about what was going on," she told the jury. "They said that he was arrested for abduction, I think, and that I had to come with them."

Gashus was questioned but never charged. Sandeson was initially arrested for kidnapping, trafficking, and misleading police, but the next day, as evidence began to emerge, he was charged with first-degree murder.

CHAPTER 6
PREPARING FOR TRIAL

Two days after William Sandeson was charged with murder, Eugene Tan was driving back to his office in downtown Halifax after an appearance in family court, when he heard the news on the radio.

"I heard it and my first reaction was, *no, it must be same name, someone else*," he says during an interview. He called a friend who confirmed it was the same Will, but Tan still couldn't be convinced. "I said, 'That can't be right. Something's gone wrong here. That can't be right.'"

Tan, who says he was never on track to become a lawyer, was called to the bar in 1996. In high school, he says, he was scientifically and musically minded. After deciding his dream of becoming a musician wasn't practical, he attended the University of Western Ontario, where he completed a degree in neuroscience.

Although he was not on track to become a lawyer, it seems it was always meant to be that way.

"I guess when they say the apple doesn't fall very far from the tree, it doesn't," he agrees.

His father was a Chinese man living in Singapore at a time when civil rights were in the forefront and was part of a movement that was trying to establish greater civil rights and also defend the existing Chinese culture in Singapore when it was being increasingly repressed. After witnessing friends and family thrown in jail, Tan's father decided he couldn't stay any longer.

"He was quite an activist, through all his days," says Tan.

Together with his mother, Tan's father began roaming the globe before settling in Guelph, Ontario, where Tan was raised. He says his father, a professor, was always community minded. It would inspire Tan to apply for law school at a time when he was trying to determine his path in life.

"I always had this sense of justice, which over time, I realized was a little bit different than all my friends," he says.

He and his wife, who is also a lawyer, have called Halifax home since 1996. He spent his first ten years practising civil litigation, personal injury and corporate law, but he was always fascinated by criminal law and aspired to argue exactly the kind of case William Sandeson presented.

But that day in August 2015 when he heard Sandeson had been arrested, he called Sandeson's father, only as a family friend. Michael Sandeson also didn't seem to know much about what was happening, but called Tan back not long after and told him his son wanted to see him. Tan went to Halifax provincial court on Spring Garden Road.

"[Will] was really bewildered at that point, had no idea what was going on," says Tan.

Tan told him he didn't know anything about what had happened either, but could try to find out. He says there was no discussion about what had happened during that first meeting and he didn't ask.

"I think he just wanted to know that there would be somebody with some knowledge who he knew who could potentially be out there, and who might also be able to answer some questions in the long run for his parents," he says.

A couple of days later, Tan got a call asking if he would take on the case. He handled the matter on his own for the bail hearing and the lengthy preliminary inquiry, at which point, Brad Sarson, managing lawyer for criminal law for Nova Scotia Legal Aid, offered to be his second chair.

"Eugene really did not look physically well," Sarson says, referencing the intense workload associated with the case.

He offered to help, and Tan jumped at the chance.

"Brad is among the best lawyers I know," says Tan. "He'll never tell you that, but he is truly among the best criminal lawyers I know."

Sarson, who was born and raised in Bedford, a suburb of Halifax, wanted to be a criminal lawyer from about the age of nine. He considered becoming a cop, a teacher, and a doctor, but eventually, after about a year and a half of practising family law, he would indeed become a criminal lawyer.

Despite eighteen years in criminal law under his belt, William Sandeson's case was the first murder he took to trial, which he attributes to the fact legal aid used to have a policy that allowed people charged with murder to choose their own counsel. That policy changed in 2014.

Sarson could not have picked a more high-profile, labour-intensive case in Nova Scotia—a case which would eventually involve surprise witnesses, calls for a mistrial, and a private investigator who would end up working against the team that had hired him. It was a trial that involved society's most desirable cohort—people who were young, attractive, and from all appearances, headed for success.

Susan MacKay was first assigned the case for the Crown. MacKay, a veteran prosecutor who had been practising for twenty-three years at the time, was born in Cape Breton and had arrived in Halifax around the same time as Eugene Tan. As the lead Crown on the case, she brought on Kim McOnie as second chair. McOnie, a Halifax native, had eighteen years under her belt, and was in her tenth year with the Crown office after working with legal aid in both Nova Scotia and Calgary.

As the evidence was trickling in, both legal teams set about preparing the case.

The first major proceeding in his case was the bail hearing, which took place in the fall of 2015, when Sandeson had been incarcerated for just over two months at the Central Nova Scotia Correctional Facility, a provincial jail in Dartmouth and Nova Scotia's largest. It houses provincially sentenced offenders, those on remand— incarcerated for things like parole suspensions and immigration violations—and newly sentenced federal offenders who are awaiting transfer to a federal penitentiary. Commonly known as the Burnside jail, it has been plagued by violence with both guards and other inmates being attacked.

And so it was that Will Sandeson wanted out. On October 21, the parties gathered in Nova Scotia Supreme Court on Halifax's Lower Water Street, with Justice Jamie Campbell presiding. At the time everything discussed and all evidence presented was subject to a publication ban. As is typically the case, it was lifted once the trial jury was sequestered.

In most circumstances, the onus is on the Crown to show why a person should be detained pending trial, but the Criminal Code recognizes that an allegation of murder is different. Because Sandeson was charged with murder, he had to show cause as to why he should be released.

Detective Constable James Wasson, the lead ident officer in the case, and Detective Constable Kim Robinson, the lead investigator at the time, both provided a sample of the evidence, which was already extensive, that police had collected so far. They admitted they still hadn't found the body and that DNA evidence was still being analyzed.

The defence also had two witnesses, their client's parents, Michael and Laurie Sandeson.

PARENTS "ALL IN"

It was late afternoon on October 22 when Michael Sandeson took the stand in what was obviously an emotional time for all of the Sandesons including William, who cried while his parents testified.

"Mr. Sandeson, you're familiar with what brings your son before the court, are you?" Eugene Tan began his questioning.

"Yes," replied Michael Sandeson.

"And you've got some knowledge about the allegations against your son?"

"Yes," he replied again, before testifying that despite that knowledge, he was putting himself forward to be a surety for his son, pledging to guarantee he would not leave the country, would report to court on time, and would be watched always.

It quickly became clear that this was a man who had no prior experience with the criminal justice system. Michael and Laurie Sandeson appeared to be a typical middle-aged couple. She with short blond hair passed on to her boys, he with dark hair and a moustache. They appeared in court together, well dressed, supporting their son in any way they could.

Michael Sandeson explained to the court that he drives a delivery truck three to four days a week, and spends the rest of his time looking after the livestock, fixing machinery at home, doing household chores, and taking care of his other sons who still live at home.

"Let's talk about the relationship between you and your son. Are you able to describe that relationship?"

"I guess, in a nutshell, we love each other."

He told the court he would talk to his son once or twice a week since he went away to university in Halifax.

"Mr. Sandeson, you understand that the charges of which he stands accused are extremely serious?"

"Yes."

"Okay, and you also understand that, in addition to these charges, there are allegations that he's been involved in some other wrongdoing, including the drug trade. Are you familiar with that?"

"Yes."

"Now what, if anything, is your knowledge of his involvement in this kind of behaviour?"

"I had no knowledge until I got a phone call after he got arrested."

He also didn't have any cause for suspicion.

"Mr. Sandeson, I wonder if you could tell the court a little bit about the authority you have over your son. How would you describe that?"

"He was always very obedient. I was able to discuss stuff with him and he could see some logic in anything that I wanted to discuss with him as long as I had a logical argument."

Michael Sandeson told the court he would put William to work on the farm and they would work side by side so that he could watch him at all times. He had also made arrangements with his part-time employer.

"If need be, he can come with me on my delivery days," said Michael Sandeson. "The other option would be that I would quit the job and stay home to make sure he's watched."

"When you say that you would quit your job, are you able to financially do that?" asked Tan.

"It would be stressful, but that would mean I could get more work done at home," Sandeson replied.

"And you said it's a possibility. How willing are you to do that, sir?"

"Well, I'll have to do it if that's what pleases the court to do, well, I'll have to do it."

Eugene Tan also presented the court with the Sandesons' property assessment, continuing a series of personal, probing questions, all with the intention of helping their son. Sandeson's father explained that their property is assessed at $264,000 for the house, $115,900 for the barn and $15,200 for the pasture land. He testified he also has a number of other small parcels of land, valued at $100,000, and that the family had a small mortgage with the Farm Loan Board, but they owed less than a $1,000 against it.

Then Tan asked him about the history of the land.

"My wife and I bought it from my parents in 1994, I believe it was. And before that, my father owned the property, and before that my grandfather was the first person to own the property in our family."

"So you're third-generation owners?"

"I'm a third-generation owner."

"Did you grow up on that piece of property, sir?"

"I grew up on that property, yes. We built our home on a corner of the property. The old original farmhouse is still there that I grew up in."

"So let me ask you, as far as your feelings or your attachment to that particular property, how would you describe that?"

"It's home. It's the only home I've ever known."

After doing the math that the Sandeson's owned roughly $440,000 of property, Eugene Tan asked the question that would illustrate just how far they were willing to go in support of their eldest son.

"Mr. Sandeson, if I were to ask you how much you would be prepared to risk, how much essentially you'd be prepared to bet on your son, is there a figure that you'd be prepared to offer?"

"I guess I'd have to say we're all in," he said, as though there were no other possible answer.

"And you understand what that might mean, sir?"

"If he messes up, we're out of a home."

"Now sir, I wonder do you happen to know if your son, has he ever expressed to you any particular connection with this property?"

"He'd like to live there someday."

His father explained he and Will had talked about making a portion of the property into an athletic field.

"He really loved the old farmhouse; he said, 'Someday I'd like that as my house when Grammy goes.'"

Tan switched gears, asking Michael Sandeson whether he was aware of his son's financial resources. His father explained that when Will was accepted into medical school, his son got a line of credit at the bank and that it was currently higher than his parents had anticipated.

"There's more drawn on it than what we thought would be education need at this time."

But the elder Sandeson said his son told him he had spent some of the money on med-school application fees, which he hadn't realized were so expensive, and that he'd invested in stocks at CIBC.

He continued that his wife was the co-signer on the line of credit, but they agreed it needed to be closed. He also told the court his son's passport was in the basement of his home and he was prepared to deliver it to the court to ensure his son could not leave the country should he be released from jail.

"Mr. Sandeson, have you ever known your son to have been in trouble, in legal trouble, in the past?"

"No. Other than parking tickets."

"Thank you Mr. Sandeson. Those are my questions."

Then it was Susan MacKay's turn to cross-examine Michael Sandeson.

"My friend has...suggested that you know about the allegations, but it's not clear to me what you do know about the allegations. So, I'm going to ask you a few questions," she began. "Are you aware that your son is alleged to have had arranged a drug deal for twenty pounds of marijuana with a street value of about $90,000?"

"I didn't know the street value. I was made aware that there was a drug deal," Sandeson replied.

"That's all you were made aware of? You didn't know how much?" MacKay challenged.

"No," came the reply.

"And are you aware the allegation is that your son shot the victim at, basically, within his own apartment in Halifax?" The cross-examination was blunt.

"I've been made aware of that, yes."

"You've been made aware of that," MacKay echoed. "Sir, you work outside the home, you say part-time, three days a week. Correct?"

"Yes."

"Sometimes four, depending on the week?"

"Sometimes four," the father agreed. "It depends if there's too much for one load on one day, they split and go another day."

He agreed with the Crown that he had three other sons who were financially dependent on him and his wife, and that while his wife also worked outside the home, they also relied on his income to support their family. He further agreed that the traditional family farm could not entirely support the family.

"Not at the lifestyle that we want to live," Sandeson told the court.

"Sure. So basically you're saying that you would be prepared to put your whole livelihood on the line for him, because if he was to get out and you were ordered to take him with you—you'd quit your job if you had to, but if something happened you'd be left with nothing, in fact, no farm, and if you quit your job, you'd have no job."

"Mm-hmm," was all that Michael Sandeson could mutter.

MacKay pointed out that Sandeson now had less contact with his son than when he was living at home, that his son was a smart young man, and at this point did what he wanted to do when he wanted to do it, giving his father no ability to exercise control over him.

"He's an adult," Sandeson agreed.

Susan MacKay then questioned Michael Sandeson about his son's line of credit, which would become all-important evidence as the case progressed.

"Sir, are you aware of how much is on the line of credit at present?" she asked.

"Approximately $78,000."

"Approximately $78,000? Okay. And, even though medical-school fees are expensive, I take it they're nowhere close to $78,000 to apply, correct?"

Sandeson said his son also used part of that money, roughly $30,000, to pay for the semester he did at Saba University. According to the school's website, tuition for the first semester of med school is $16,000, plus other student fees, travel, and accommodation. In 2015, first-year medical school at Dal cost $19,440, including tuition for two semesters and other student fees.

"So you agree with me, sir, that your son was acting on his own in deciding that he was going to, as he told you, invest money from that line of credit? He wasn't doing that in consultation with you or your wife, to your knowledge, correct?" MacKay continued with the line of questioning, seemingly intended to illustrate Michael Sandeson would not be able to control his son's every move as he was suggesting.

"He asked me what I thought about borrowing money to invest to make more. And I said it's a little risky, but if the interest rates are low and you can put it some place pretty secure, then there's a benefit to it in the longer run."

The cross-examination concluded with Sandeson telling the court his wife's salary was $80,000, with him earning an additional $30,000 from his part-time job.

Then it was his wife's turn.

"Okay, Ms. Sandeson, I'll get right to the point," Eugene Tan began. "You're familiar with why your son is currently in custody?"

"Yes I am," she responded.

"I wonder if you might be able to describe for me your understanding, generally, of the allegations against your son?"

"First-degree murder charge, that's what I understand."

"So, what does that mean to you?"

"It's about the worst charge anybody could have, from what I understand."

"Let's talk about your relationship. First let's just talk about the relationship between parent and child. How would you describe your relationship with William?"

"I've been very proud of William for the accomplishments that he's made in his relatively short life. Love my son, just as I love all my other boys."

"In terms of parental authority, or really any authority, how would you describe your ability to control his behaviour or hold him accountable for his behaviour?"

"Well certainly, when he lived under our roof, we held him accountable and he lived by our rules. When he went off to university, we gave him advice on how to cope away from home. And I mean he was certainly back and forth—it wasn't that far away from Truro. And then when he became an adult and went off to the Caribbean for instance, that was a pretty big leap for a young man to do, and we got a sense he was doing okay."

William Sandeson's parents obviously had no idea he wasn't doing okay, not okay at all.

As he did with her husband, Tan asked Laurie Sandeson about the property on which she lives with her family.

"Is there an emotional connection at all?" he questioned.

"Oh, I grew up on a farm in PEI, and I was happy to marry a farmer and live in Truro, and happy to be on the farm again."

Then back to the money.

"What knowledge have you got about that line of credit?"

"Receive a monthly statement because I'm a guarantor on that line of credit, so I see the monthly statements."

Mrs. Sandeson said her son would have qualified for the line of credit without her if he had needed a line of credit in Canada, but because he was leaving the country, the bank needed somebody in Canada to be the guarantor. She said she became concerned about the line of credit back in the spring.

"I noticed that the line of credit had jumped from about $25,000 to about forty-some-thousand, so I was concerned."

"Okay. So, did you act on that concern?"

"Yes. I confronted William right away, and I was concerned. I said, 'I don't understand why this jumped that high,' and he explained to me the reasons why it had gone up.

"So what were his reasons, ma'am?"

"Just that...because the line-of-credit interest rate was so low, he thought if he borrowed on that to make investments that would work, would make more money...And he was talking to somebody at CIBC about what smart investments looked like at that point in time."

His mother said she and her husband had given William a name of a person he could meet with at the CIBC in Halifax.

"Ms. Sandeson, do you know what it means to be a surety?"

"Caretaker? Kind of supervisor?"

"Do you understand what your role is to be or your obligations are?"

"Yes. You have to ensure the terms of the bail are met."

"Ms. Sandeson, you're working so you're not able to be home during the day. Your husband is able to be home. If your husband were to leave his job, his part-time job as a driver, how would you feel about that?"

"We'd be okay. We might have to let some things go in terms of lifestyle habits, but we'd be okay."

"Let's talk about the land and the farm and whatnot, the financial value of all that. How much are you willing to bet on your son?"

"All of it," Laurie Sandeson replied, echoing her husband's earlier testimony.

Eugene Tan argued Sandeson should be released into the custody of his parents on a bond of $100,000, but reiterated the parents would be willing to pledge in excess of $400,000 if the court wished.

"That would likely be the largest bond that certainly I've come across in similar circumstances," said Tan pointing out that Dennis Oland, who was charged with the second-degree murder of his father, Richard Oland, in New Brunswick, was released on bail with a $50, 000 bond.

Sandeson was, in fact, so desperate to get out of jail that his lawyer argued he wasn't even asking for the three to four hours a week of personal time that people seeking bail often request. Tan argued the file was going to go on for a matter of years and would not be proceeding to trial anytime soon, noting disclosure had just been received and contained several thousand pages, that a preliminary inquiry alone would take weeks, and dates had not even been set, let alone for a trial, which hadn't even yet been thought about.

"Mr. Sandeson has a Charter right, a basic entitlement to be granted reasonable bail unless there is just cause to do otherwise," Tan argued.

The Crown, in turn, pointed to the significant amount of evidence the police had already amassed in the two months since Taylor Samson had disappeared, including forensic DNA evidence, physical evidence, photographic evidence, electronic evidence, and the accused's own numerous self-contradictory statements to the police.

There are three grounds under which lawyers can argue to keep people who have been charged with an offence in jail. In this case, the Crown argued it could meet all three. Susan MacKay told the court the Crown was worried Sandeson was a flight risk, that detaining him was necessary to ensure the protection and safety of the public, and to maintain public confidence in the administration of justice.

But in the end the decision was Justice Jamie Campbell's.

BAIL DENIED

The judge began by acknowledging the accused was about to enter Dalhousie Medical School at the time of the alleged crime.

It's reasonable to infer that he is of above-average intelligence and perhaps that he's not afraid of hard work. He comes from a hard-working farm family in Lower Truro. He has three younger brothers who apparently look up to him.

Will Sandeson has no criminal record. Unlike many people who appear in bail hearings, there's just no criminal record at all. His family, it seems, would be far removed from the world where criminal records are the norm. He grew up in a normal, middle-class, *rural Nova Scotia family. They made trips to Florida, and he was able to travel overseas on a few occasions. No one had the slightest idea that William Sandeson was a dope dealer. The evidence of his involvement in drugs is so strong as to be overwhelming. And the evidence is that he was more than just a petty street-level dealer. He was dealing with at least one shipment of twenty pounds, apparently having a street value of about $90,000. He was running with some very dangerous people. It's not the kind of world that his farm family could even have imagined.*

Campbell noted that just because Sandeson had no criminal record, that didn't necessarily mean he had never been involved in a crime, just that he had never been caught. He said:

The evidence is substantial that he was a drug dealer who had, to this point, evaded detection. There's an old saying that there is no honour among thieves. There's none among drug dealers either. Dangerous people are part of that life, and nice guys don't succeed.

Will Sandeson was not, it is evident, the kind of person whom his parents believed him to be. He was involved in a drug business where, if he had been caught, he would have found himself spending some years in jail rather than going to med school. He is a high risk–taker.

There's some evidence as well to suggest that he is impetuous. His response to his girlfriend's cheating on him was to threaten to kill her and dispose of her body. Smart people don't usually say those kind of things to others unless they're very much caught up in a moment.

Campbell was referencing unsettling evidence presented in the bail hearing by then lead investigator Detective Constable Kim Robinson. Robinson had told the court that five or six weeks prior to the murder of Taylor Samson, Sandeson had been upset that his girlfriend had cheated on him. In a text to another friend, he said that he would kill her and discard of her body at the back of his parents' property, so that coyotes could get it. He also mentioned he would cut off her head and her hands and put them in a bucket of lye.

Lye is a metal hydroxide most commonly used to cure many types of food and make soap. It can also be used to digest tissues of animal carcasses by placing the body in a sealed chamber, adding a mixture of lye and water, and applying heat to accelerate the process. After several hours the substance will take on a coffee-like appearance, with the only solids remaining very fragile bone hulls, which can be mechanically crushed to a fine powder with very little force.

"Rather than realizing that something very bad was going down and telling the police what happened, he tried to fix it," said Justice Jamie Campbell. "Either he was trying to hide evidence of his own crime, or was trying to hide evidence of someone else's crime."

Campbell said the Crown's case was a strong one, but he also acknowledged that so was the release plan Sandeson's defence team and parents were proposing. "Their confidence in him is as it should be. Parental love is not supposed to be rational, but entirely unconditional."

But the complete devotion of William Sandeson's parents would not be enough. Campbell said he was concerned Sandeson could be motivated to tamper with evidence or even intimidate witnesses, given that Taylor Samson's body still hadn't been found. Campbell said:

No one knows what cash he might have or what contacts he might have...He knows he's facing a strong case and a potential twenty-five-year jail term. He would be eligible for parole sometime in his late forties. He is a person who is prepared to take high-level risks. He lived a risky lifestyle. He's prepared to act without giving matters much thought. He would be highly motivated to make an attempt to escape, intellectually capable of devising a plan to flee without a passport, and impetuous enough to potentially try it.

Judge Jamie Campbell denied Sandeson's application for bail.

"Public confidence in the system of justice would not be maintained if a person accused of a drug trade–related handgun murder, in which the evidence and the body of the victim were disposed of by means unknown, facing a strong Crown case and the potential of life in prison, were released to his parents' home where, incidentally, the evidence suggests the cleanup materials from a killing were hidden," he ruled.

No sooner had the judge left the courtroom than Taylor Samson's mother called out, "Maybe you'll do one decent thing for your fucking family and give my son back to me!"

There was no response.

William Sandeson would remain behind bars until the start of his trial a year and seven months later. The lawyers were likely not aware at the time, but the case would become the lengthiest matter they had ever handled.

CHAPTER 7
THE CROWN'S CASE: FAMILY FIRST

O
n April 20, 2017, Crown Attorney Susan MacKay stood in courtroom 301 in Nova Scotia Supreme Court introducing herself and her co-counsel, Kim McOnie. William Sandeson had been behind bars for one year, eight months, and two days. MacKay wasted no time in addressing the jury directly.

"No doubt you've all seen TV shows like *Matlock, Law & Order, L.A. Law,* maybe, if you're as old as I am," she joked. "Or maybe even *Perry Mason.* Well, those shows can offer good entertainment, but what happens in courtrooms like this one is not quite as smooth as what you see on TV or Netflix."

She was certainly correct in that the trial that was about to ensue would be anything but smooth. Riddled with delays and interruptions, it stretched on for two months, making it one of the longest trials in the province's history.

Blair Rhodes, a veteran Nova Scotia reporter, had been covering courts off and on for thirty-seven years and had been dedicated almost exclusively to court coverage for the CBC for six. He's seen his share of high-profile murder trials. He says this one spiralled out of control—so much so that the judge appeared to be exasperated as he tried to protect the jury.

"It's the worst trial I've seen in that respect—the number of interruptions. It was like they were getting hammered from all sides."

MacKay explained to the jury that the Crown had the burden of presenting the evidence necessary to find Sandeson guilty and that he did not have to prove his innocence. "He is presumed innocent unless, and until, you decide otherwise," she told the eight men and eight women gathered before her. [Two of them were alternates and would be dismissed before the first witness was called. Two more would leave before the jury began deliberating. Only twelve could decide the case as per the Criminal Code of Canada.]

The monumental task before them had to be setting in. They would either put a killer behind bars and give a young man's family justice, or leave that family searching for answers and set a young doctor free potentially to save hundreds of lives. It was up to them.

"While this task may be a bit nerve-racking, all that's required is your eyes, your ears, and your good common sense," said MacKay.

Then, so there could be no question, she read them the charge:

"William Michael Sandeson stands charged that he, on or about August 15, 2015, at or near Halifax in the county of Halifax in the province of Nova Scotia, did unlawfully cause the death of Taylor Samson and did thereby commit first-degree murder."

She explained that there are central elements that the Crown must prove—that the murder took place within the province of Nova Scotia, the date on which it occurred, that William Sandeson was responsible, and that the first-degree murder of Taylor Samson actually took place. MacKay also explained that in order to be first-degree murder, the killing must be planned and deliberate.

"These elements are like pieces of a puzzle that come together to found the charge," she explained. "Each piece will come together from all the evidence presented in the Crown's case, which we submit will form the clear picture of William Sandeson's guilt beyond a reasonable doubt."

Samson's mother, whose presence at the trial never wavered, sat with some of his friends who were there as much as they could be, on one side of the courtroom's public gallery. Samson's step-mother and stepsister were also present. Sandeson's family was not present. (They later said they did not attend because they believed they were not allowed as they may have been called to testify. The Crown later said that was not the case.) Members of the media sat together, filling several rows of seating, on the other side of the courtroom.

The trial attracted a large media presence, more even than other Halifax murder trials, with most outlets committing resources to cover each and every day. Media outlets, especially smaller ones with fewer resources, often cover only the first and last days of the trial, but even the most under-resourced newsrooms in Halifax committed to Sandeson's murder trial.

SAMSON'S MOTHER TAKES THE STAND

The Crown's first witness was Taylor Samson's mother, Linda Boutilier. Boutilier told the jury she had last heard from her son on a Thursday, that he had texted to say he would be going home to Amherst for a visit the following Sunday, but he didn't arrive.

She testified she was very close with her son and saw him on a regular basis. She said sometimes he would go home once a week, but sometimes she wouldn't see him for a month. Even then, they would talk on the phone or text.

"I'd call him and say, 'Whatcha been up to?' Sometimes he would just message me and say, 'I love you mom.'"

"And were you aware of whether Taylor had any future plans?" MacKay asked.

"He planned on getting his doctorate in physics," Boutilier replied before being cut off by Eugene Tan.

"I'm going to object, my lord," he said, getting to his feet.

The judge asked the jury to leave.

"Not sure that that question is probative in any way. It's not relevant and it seems designed to elicit some form of emotional response," Tan continued.

"M'lord, the defence has indicated in the past that they don't concede that Taylor Samson is dead," argued MacKay. "We are attempting to elicit evidence that might show that if he had been alive he would be in touch with his mother."

"They haven't objected to any of the information regarding communications," said Justice Arnold.

"We'll withdraw the question," MacKay conceded after conferring with her co-counsel, Kim McOnie.

It would be the first of many objections that saw the jury entering and exiting the courtroom.

"When did you first become aware that Taylor Samson, your son, was missing?" continued MacKay when the jury was once again seated before them.

"The following Sunday, August 16, around five o'clock. Connor, my younger son, and I were up getting groceries and we were walking home and Connor got a message through messenger on Facebook from his father saying, 'Just wanted to let you know, Taylor's been missing since last night.'"

"So what did you do when you heard about this?" MacKay asked.

"I went right home, I called a few friends to find out if they'd seen him because I knew that Taylor was coming up on Sunday to pick up a friend of his that had been out West. He was going to bring him down to Halifax and it was going to be after a ball game."

Boutilier testified she got on the phone and started messaging people on Facebook, before going to Halifax that night. She arrived around 11:30.

"I called the police officer that was handling the missing person case, and honestly I don't remember the whole conversation 'cause it was a long time ago and I was still in a panic," she testified. "Then I started searching."

Together with one of Taylor's friends, she walked the streets, up and down sidewalks, looking under bushes and in dumpsters. The next morning, she went to the police station and gave a statement.

"I wanted to tell the police that I knew it was more than just a missing person, that something had happened to my son. I felt something had happened to my son because he had no contact with anybody within twenty-four hours."

"And did you consider that yourself, to be unusual for your son?"

"Very unusual."

But later that evening, Boutilier gave another statement.

"I believe I had more information that I had heard that I wanted to give to the police," she told the jury.

The Crown did not ask her what that information was.

"At any point in time, were you contacted by the police in regard to providing a sample for DNA analysis?"

Boutilier confirmed that she was.

"I was out searching for Taylor that day, I'm not sure which day it was. I got a call from [an officer] and asked me to come back to Taylor's apartment where we were staying, with his brother, they wanted to get a blood sample from both of us."

Susan MacKay produced two photos and asked Linda Boutilier if she recognized the person.

"That's Taylor, my son."

"Do you know who that is?" MacKay asked, pointing to the next photo.

"Taylor, my son," Boutilier responded, but her voice broke and she started to cry.

"Thank you Ms. Boutilier. Those are my questions for you."

But now it was Brad Sarson's turn, and he wasted no time.

"One thing Ms. MacKay did not touch upon was Taylor's involvement in selling drugs, and my understanding is that you were aware that at the very least, when Taylor moved to Halifax, when he started university, he began selling marijuana?"

"Yes," she replied.

"And you were aware of this, he didn't hide that fact from you. Correct?"

"I was aware; I didn't like it, but I was aware, yeah."

"Right. And he was supporting himself somewhat through student loans?"

"Through student loans and other things that he was doing, yes."

"Right. But he was selling marijuana for some spending money?"

"Yes, and other things, yes."

"Did you know who Taylor's supplier was?"

"No."

"Did you know who Taylor was selling to?

"A few, yes."

"A few, as in you knew their names or you knew them personally?"

"I knew their names and a few I knew personally."

"You also were under the impression that Taylor was only selling small quantities of marijuana, correct?"

"Yes."

"In fact, you believed that he was only selling gram amounts to friends, maybe occasionally as much as an ounce of marijuana?"

"Yes."

"And I think it'd be fair to say that when you learned initially at least that you were under the belief that he had four pounds of marijuana to sell on the night of August 15, you were shocked, weren't you?"

"Yes, I was."

"And that was far beyond any quantity of drug that you thought that he would ever be involved in, correct?"

"Yes."

"I'm guessing that you later learned that the quantity of marijuana that he had with him that night was not four pounds, but was twenty pounds, correct?"

"Yes, in court I did, yes."

In a series of questions, Sarson asked Boutilier whether it would be news to her that her son was involved in either the sale or possession of mushrooms, cocaine, MDMA or ecstasy, or prescription drugs, indicating police had information he was. In all cases, she responded that it would indeed be news to her.

"Another thing that didn't come up when Ms. MacKay was asking you some questions was with respect to Taylor's medical condition. My understanding was that around the age of fifteen it was discovered that he had an autoimmune disease of some sort that affected his liver."

"Autoimmune liver disease, yes," she responded, explaining that he was taking daily medication.

"You also shared with the police the fact that not having his medication for a couple of days wouldn't present any serious difficulties for him, correct?" Sarson was setting the scene to argue that police had no urgent need to burst into Sandeson's apartment without a warrant.

"I said to two different officers two different things really."

"Okay. Do you remember what you told the officers?"

"The first one I told, I remember saying that if he had no alcohol into him that he could go three or four, sometimes a week. I think the other officer I told him three or four days before it actually started affecting his liver, if he didn't take his medication."

"And is that the extent of what you remember telling the police?"

"To my knowledge, yes, because it was like seven or eight o'clock that night when I started giving the second statement and I had been without sleep for over thirty-six hours and I was more worried about finding Taylor than anything else. I don't recall exactly what I said in those statements."

Sarson then quoted Boutilier's statement to police, asking her if she recalled saying, "After probably five or six days, his liver, the enzymes will start going up and his liver will start getting enlarged."

Boutilier said that she did.

Sarson asked her if she recalled saying, "He may not even be for a week."

"Yes, I remember that, yeah," she replied.

Sarson went on, still quoting the transcript of Boutilier's statement to police.

"'If he's out like a week or so, he'll probably start having a little bit of jaundice or whatever and I'd say within two weeks, then he could be starting vomiting up brown bile.' Do you remember saying that?"

"Yes."

In the transcript, the officer says, "But, we're talking forty-eight hours right now, so he should be okay medically wise?" Boutilier replies, "No, he's fine."

"Yes, I did say that," she agreed in court.

"Finally, Ms. Boutilier, do you recall talking to the police about Taylor having a temper?"

His mother said that she did.

Sarson read from Boutilier's statement: "'Taylor can fight. I'll tell you and everybody will tell you, Taylor can fight. Taylor, if someone is picking on one of his friends or downtown at a bar, Taylor can take on three people and put them down flat. And I'm talking like thirty-year-old guys when he was sixteen years old.'"

His mother also agreed she had said that, and then it was over.

Linda Boutilier took her seat in the public gallery, but not before the defence tried to get her kicked out of the courtroom for the duration of the trial, arguing she was disruptive and "making comments" during the bail hearing and the preliminary inquiry, and the fear of that happening again was heightened considering the case would now be in front of a jury.

Justice Arnold ruled the victim's mother should be treated like any other witness and permitted to sit in the public gallery after she had testified.

"I don't know what happened in those other courts, but...I can assure you that during this trial, there won't be anything like that tolerated at all," Arnold said in relation to Boutilier's previous outbursts.

Boutilier was present every day of the trial, even when the jury wasn't and the lawyers were making legal arguments. She was

Taylor Samson's most visible advocate and developed online followers who felt her mother's anguish. Some of them even reached out to her directly, and a couple showed up at court at various points throughout the trial. The defence needn't have worried. There were no outbursts, at least not inside the courtroom.

SAMSON'S GIRLFRIEND TESTIFIES

Taylor Samson's girlfriend, Mackenzie Ruthven, also took the stand. She was twenty-one at the time and told the jury she had just graduated from Dalhousie University with a bachelor's degree in physics with a minor in math. She started to cry as soon as she was asked where she studied.

"I'm sorry, I just need a minute," she said.

It reiterated that this trial was presenting a lineup of smart kids, all attractive and with bright futures ahead of them before they got tangled up in this mess, all in slightly different ways, some through no fault of their own.

Ruthven had been dating Samson for six months when he was killed.

"How often would you see him?" asked Susan MacKay, still handling questioning for the Crown.

"I would stay over most nights throughout the week."

"And during the day how much would you see him?"

"I was working full-time and I was in school, so I did not see him throughout the day. I would see him more at night after I was done everything I had to do that day," said Ruthven, who also testified she had been working at the Health and Safety Office at Dal.

"So, when is the last time that you recall seeing Taylor Samson?" MacKay asked.

"Saturday, August 15, 2015, at 10:30 P.M."

"And where were you when you last saw him?"

"We were at 6093 South Street in the apartment that he had just started moving into."

"And was anyone else there when you last saw him?"

"My exchange student was outside smoking, and no one else was present besides her."

"So you had an exchange student; where was she from?"

"She was from Italy."

"And when did she arrive?"

"She arrived on Thursday." That was two days before Samson was last seen.

"What were your plans for later that evening?" MacKay continued.

"He wanted to show [my exchange student] downtown so we were gonna go to Pacifico with a group of his friends," Ruthven said, referencing a downtown Halifax dance club.

"And how long were you expecting Taylor to be gone when he left?"

"He said he was just going a couple houses down and would be right back."

"And have you had any contact from him since?"

"No."

There was that ever-present issue that Samson's body had not been found, and the Crown did not want to leave any possibility for the defence to argue he wasn't dead.

"Did you try to contact him?" MacKay went on.

"Multiple times," said Ruthven.

"When did you do that?"

"That evening and multiple times after that. I tried calling him twice that evening and I tried texting him probably about seven times."

"Did you get any response from him?" the Crown asked, her voice softening.

"No."

"When he left, what did he have with him?"

"He had his cellphone and a black bag."

The Crown showed Ruthven photos and she identified Samson and the bag he was carrying.

"When he left, what did he leave behind?

"He left his wallet, his keys, and his medication."

"Those are my questions for you. The defence may have some questions for you, Ms. Ruthven."

Brad Sarson began by asking Ruthven about the three statements she had given to police, two on August 17 and one on the 18th. She admitted she was less than forthcoming with police the first time but said she gave them as much information as she could after that.

She told the jury that while they hadn't started dating until January 2015, she had actually met Samson in the summer or early fall of 2014, when she moved into his old apartment. She also admitted she had some knowledge Taylor was involved in the drug trade, but testified, "He tried very hard to hide it from me."

"So he didn't deny it, right?"

"He did." Ruthven contradicted the defence.

"Okay, initially he did?"

"Yes," agreed Ruthven.

"Okay, but eventually it became obvious that he was selling some drugs and at that point in time he just tried to sort of minimize your exposure to it, if I could put it that way?"

"Yes."

Ruthven went on to say that when Samson left the apartment that night she believed the bag he was carrying contained a fair amount of marijuana, more than she knew that Taylor was involved with selling at one time.

"You had certainly seen him with drugs before, right?" asked Sarson.

"Yes," replied Ruthven.

"And you had occasionally seen his friends come over and he would sell to them, small quantities of marijuana?"

"Yes." Her voice was quiet, almost meek.

"And although he used marijuana with the people he was selling to, he also would use cocaine on occasion, correct?"

"If we were going out or something like that, yes."

Ruthven also told Brad Sarson she was aware of Samson's auto-immune disease and that he was supposed to take his medication once a day. She told Sarson about a time he hadn't taken his meds for a couple of days and he started getting heartburn, so she went to get his prescription filled for him. Sarson asked her if Taylor could go months without the treatment, but the Crown objected, saying the question wasn't relevant and was also based on hearsay.

That was when the judge suggested Ruthven leave the court-room to compose herself while the objection was discussed. She leapt at the chance and ran out of the courtroom crying.

It was decided that the defence could proceed with the questioning about Samson's medication but only in the context of what Ruthven told police. Sarson began quoting Ruthven's earlier statement.

"The way that he's explained it to me, because I've gotten very mad at him for not taking medication before, is that it would have to be a long period of time, so a couple of months to a year in order for there to be any real discrepancy in like, his health."

Ruthven pointed out she got this information through an argument with Taylor in which he was trying to calm her down, to defuse the situation. She seemed to be implying it may have been exaggerated.

Ruthven agreed she told police a number of people were sitting around the common room at Taylor's apartment on South Street in the early morning hours of Friday, August 14. She said a person named Devon arrived and Taylor immediately took him upstairs to his bedroom. She testified that the bag Devon arrived with looked like the bag Taylor left with Saturday night, but she couldn't be sure if it was the exact bag. Ruthven didn't recall ever seeing this Devon person before, but said he did not have the black bag when he came back downstairs. He sat down briefly with the people sitting around, and there was an awkward introduction made by Taylor.

"Devon" was never actually identified.

Ruthven testified she had seen Taylor off and on throughout the day on August 15, as he had baseball and he also went to the gym. Upon questioning from Brad Sarson, she agreed Taylor was distracted or disengaged, but disagreed when it was suggested he was nervous or stressed. She said he was on his phone a lot and that he wanted to get a group of people together to go to Pacifico.

"All right, any other word you would use to describe his demeanour?" Sarson pressed.

"I believe I used the word 'antsy' before, like he wanted to just get out and go."

Sarson then asked Ruthven if she had any direct knowledge about how much money Samson made through the drug trade.

"I know that he had a list that he kept about like, if people didn't pay him right away, but that was about it. He would never tell me how much."

But Sarson quoted Ruthven's statement to the police in which she is asked if Taylor made a lot of money selling drugs and she responds, "more or less, yeah."

"What was the basis for your answer?" Sarson probed.

"That he was, from my understanding, trying to pay his way through university," Ruthven responded, agreeing with the defence that she was aware her boyfriend had a safe in the apartment and that he kept his money in it.

She said she had no knowledge of Taylor selling drugs other than marijuana but that he did act as a go-between for MDMA and 'shrooms. She wasn't sure whether he got paid for that.

Ruthven returned to the gallery.

CHAPTER 8
THE CROWN'S CASE: POLICE WORK

The work of the police would be questioned time and again throughout William Sandeson's first-degree murder trial, but the Crown presented a lineup of officers supporting their efforts.

Sergeant Tanya Chambers-Spriggs, a shift supervisor for Halifax Regional Police at the time of Taylor Samson's disappearance, testified she was one of the officers who went out to meet Linda Boutilier when she showed up at headquarters very upset.

"There was nothing initially, I guess, that stood out about his missing person report," Chambers-Spriggs testified. "The young man hadn't been seen for about a day and a half at that period of time."

But that was when Boutilier disclosed to police that her son's friends had told her he may have had marijuana with him—a significant amount. As a result, Chambers-Spriggs had Samson's phone pinged to determine its location.

It didn't work.

"We had information come back shortly after that—that the phone was either out of range or off," the officer testified.

Police were concerned about Samson's health due to his auto-immune disease and the urgency of the situation was increasing, so they asked for the last number contacted by Samson's phone. Chambers-Spriggs testified she got the number but it was a 705 number, not the 902 Nova Scotia area code police had been anticipating. Around the same time, police received some data from the CPIC (Canadian Police Information Centre) operator indicating the phone was being operated with some sort of internet-based telephone service. This was not within Chambers-Spriggs's area of expertise so she forwarded the information to Detective Constable Todd Blake.

Blake testified the cellphone number was used through a carrier called Iristel, a voice-to-internet service provider based in Ontario. Blake explained to the jury that the company has a group of phone numbers that they provide to resellers to use for different mobile applications. The 705 number that had been contacting Taylor Samson was resold to an app called Nextplus, a free web-based phone provider. Blake explained that if you have a phone or an iPad that is not set up to a cellphone contract, you can use a Wi-Fi-capable device and get a free phone number.

"You can put any name you want, you can put any date of birth you want, you can put whatever you want on there because it's not verified because it is a free application," he testified.

William Sandeson sat paying close attention and taking notes, often wearing a Dal track suit. His legal team told reporters covering the trial that he was very involved in his own defence, having read every scrap of paperwork related to the case.

Blake told the jury he wrote a production order, which he served on the internet provider, Eastlink, to get access to the IP (Internet Protocol) address, which would provide the location from which the internet was being accessed. That led him to Regional Residential Services, based on Cavalier Drive in Lower Sackville, where William Sandeson worked.

Eugene Tan rose to cross-examine Blake, but his questions were not about any of the information elicited by the Crown. Tan wanted to know about a search warrant Blake executed on Taylor Samson's apartment in the back of the frat house on South Street. Tan produced the evidence-processing sheet completed during the search.

Blake confirmed the list, explaining that he and another officer seized 185.5 grams of marijuana, four cellphones, a digital scale, Samson's passport, a tin case containing $1,680 in Canadian currency, and a safe containing several more envelopes of money totalling $6,350 Canadian and $20 American.

"They were all very neat; it was a very tidy set, and each of these envelopes had the writings, which I have marked on there, 'Blue Dream,' 'Diesel,' 'wr,' 'og,'" testified Blake.

Blake didn't testify as to the meaning of the labels, but a Google search indicates they refer to particular strains of marijuana. "wr" stands for "White Rhino," "og," or "og Kush" as it is more commonly known, stands for either "Ocean Grown" or "Original Gangster."

"All right. Now as I understand it, all of these items were located in one single room, is that right?" Eugene Tan pressed on.

"That's correct," responded Blake.

"And in fact, the frat had given it a name, it was a memorial room of some kind, do you recall? Memorial smoking room or something like that?"

"I can honestly say I've never heard that."

A friend of the frat confirmed to the author there was indeed a room at Sigma Chi dubbed the "memorial" smoking room as a joke after the brother who lived there left. It was essentially just a room the brothers used for smoking, and the name stuck even after others moved in.

The purpose of the testimony seemed to be to further establish that Taylor Samson used and sold drugs.

Tan moved on.

"It doesn't appear in the exhibit log and I don't believe it's in your notes, but did you at any time come across a prescription bottle for Taylor Samson?"

"No, I don't recall a prescription, no."

Tan was again setting himself up to argue that Taylor Samson didn't need his meds as urgently as had been suggested and therefore police had no right to burst into his client's apartment searching for Samson.

THE EVIDENCE COLLECTED

At this point in the trial, the lawyers whipped through testimony of various police officers fairly quickly. Detective Constable Randy Wood testified he was with HRP's General Investigations Sections at the time and was one of the officers who attended William Sandeson's workplace after police connected the address to Taylor Samson through phone records.

Sergeant Bobby Clyke testified he was brought in on August 17.

"First, I reached out to some confidential informants to see if we could ascertain any information on missing person Taylor Samson," he told the jury.

When that didn't turn up anything, he accompanied Detective Constable Wood to Lower Sackville.

Sergeant Charla Keddy testified she was the one who took William Sandeson's first statement, when he was still considered a witness, not a suspect.

But it was Sergeant Sandra Johnston who would give the jury the first glimpse into just how much evidence police had compiled against William Sandeson.

Johnston told the court she had been a police officer for twenty-five years. In August 2015, she was in the Forensic Identification

Section with Halifax Regional Police. She was called to William Sandeson's apartment on Henry Street on August 17 to photograph a bag that had been located outside the building.

"What did it contain?" asked Susan MacKay.

"It contained four one-litre bottles of formamide," replied Johnston. "They were unopened." Formamide is an industrial chemical, a clear liquid with an ammonia-like odour, used in the manufacturing of pharmaceuticals, herbicides, pesticides, and other chemical substances.

Johnston seized the items and took them back to police head-quarters. She went back and forth to the Henry Street apartment three times two days later, staying for most of the day.

"I arrived at 5:26 A.M. until 12:07, then I returned at 3:06 P.M. I left at 6:30 P.M. I returned at 8:20 P.M. and I left at 9:10 P.M.," Johnston testified with precision.

It was still dark when she arrived and there were officers stationed outside in an unmarked police car.

"I went into the apartment. When you go in, the entrance is on the east side, which is on Henry Street. You go up two flights of stairs and down a hallway. The scene was a two-bedroom apartment," Johnston told the jury.

Two officers who had been guarding the apartment overnight left as Johnston entered the apartment alone.

"I put booties on, which are the large slippers, Tyvek booties that go up to your knees," Johnston continued.

"What did you notice when you went in there?" questioned MacKay.

"The apartment was neat."

Johnston testified she then photographed and videotaped the scene with the assistance of Detective Constable Rob Furlong who arrived at 5:45. They began processing the scene at 6:00 A.M.

"We examined the scene looking for anything that would be related to evidence as to what happened to Mr. Samson," Johnston said. "I located some blood spatter in the bathroom near the floor."

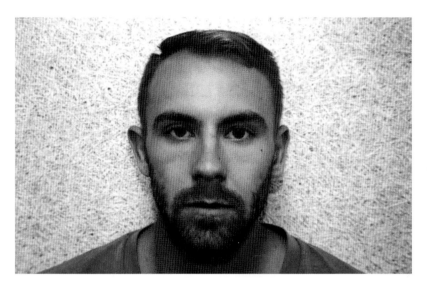

TOP: A Will Sandeson mugshot taken by a Halifax Regional Police officer shortly after the Dalhousie medical student was charged with murder. BOTTOM: Will Sandeson (foreground) and Taylor Samson in the hallway of Sandeson's building. The surveillance tape is dated 08/15/2015, 22:26.00, and Samson is carrying a black duffle bag. Samson was never seen on camera leaving the building.

15·09·02
Fil.#15-115511

TOP: A surveillance tape shows Sandeson and his girlfriend, Sonja Gashus, dated 08/15/2015, 20:49.25, heading to his apartment. Sandeson appears to be carrying a pizza box. Gashus testified that she left the apartment and then received a text from Will at 12:30 A.M., telling her she could return. *BOTTOM:* One of the bloodstained twenty-dollar bills found in Will Sandeson's apartment.

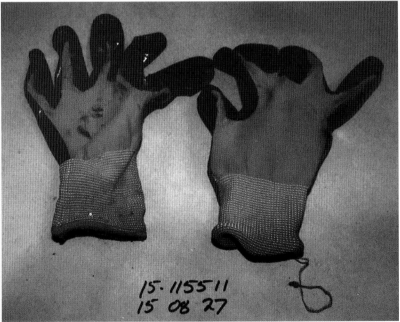

15. 115511
15 08 27

TOP: A Smith & Wesson SD9, an exhibit at the murder trial. The jury was shown a gun, bullets, and cash seized from Sandeson's apartment.
BOTTOM: Gloves entered into the trial as evidence.

ABOVE: Recovered bags of weed. The court was told that on August 15, 2015, Taylor Samson went to Will Sandeson's downtown Halifax apartment to sell nine kilograms of marijuana for $40,000 as part of a prearranged deal.

LEFT: Taylor Samson and his girlfriend, Mackenzie Ruthven. She testified she was in a relationship with Samson for about six months before he disappeared.

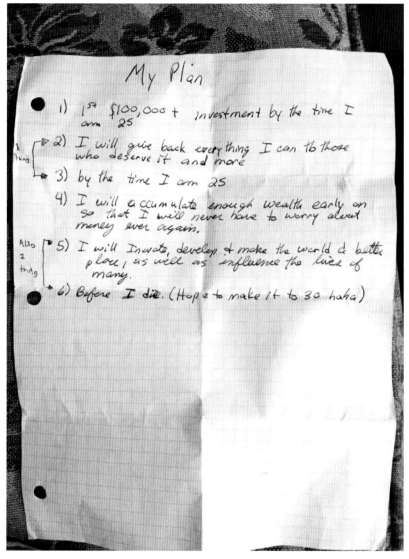

A plan that Taylor Samson had made for his life. By the time, he was twenty-five he wanted "to accumulate enough wealth early on so that I will never have to worry about money ever again." Ominously, he also wrote, "Hope to make it to 30 haha."

Will Sandeson photographed by police. On the floor is a photograph of Taylor Samson and his brother, Connor, used by police during their interrogation.

The exterior of the South End Halifax building where Sandeson lived, not far from Dalhousie Medical School, where was scheduled to start classes.

The crime scene. In the trial's most shocking twist, two of Sandeson's track teammates testified that they went to Sandeson's apartment after hearing a gunshot. There they saw a body slumped over in a chair, bleeding. They would become the trial's star witnesses.

The Crown provided a book of Johnston's photographs to the jury and the officer began detailing what she had captured in each one. Johnston described exterior shots of the apartment building on Henry Street, the grocery bag from Pete's Fine Foods containing the formamide, and the stairs leading to the apartment.

"Do you see, in the top corner, a round black circle? Do you know what that is?" MacKay interjected.

"Yes, that's a security camera," answered Johnston, before moving on to the next photo. That camera, and the video it was recording, would become critical evidence.

Johnston described a view looking through the open door of apartment two, looking directly into the kitchen and dining room area, showing a table and two chairs and a black silhouette that Johnston said was a shooting target on the door.

There were photos of the hallway going to the bathroom, the toilet, the tub, garbage can, closets, the kitchen, and each of the bedrooms.

"Sixteen is an overall of the north bedroom, and the screen is removed from the window and it's laying on top of the bed," Johnston said, counting her way through the numbered photos.

She explained that after the apartment was photographed and videotaped, she and her partner began examining the scene.

"I found blood spatter in the bathroom and it was marked with alphabetical stickers," Johnston continued.

But Eugene Tan was on his feet.

"Sorry, m'lord," he interjected.

"What appeared to be blood spatter," Sergeant Johnston corrected herself.

"I just wanted to clarify that point and Sergeant Johnston made a reference earlier to blood, and I think it would be appropriate to clarify whether what she observed at the time was what she knew was blood or what she believed to be blood," Tan said, making the point that when Johnston was at the scene in those very early days the substance had not yet been tested.

"So you believed it to be blood?" Susan MacKay continued questioning.

"Yes," agreed the officer, before returning to the book of photos, now providing detail on the spots that appeared to have been blood spatter.

"That's the left-hand side of the doorjamb to the bathroom on the floor," she explained, going through dozens of photographs showing stickers marking areas she believed to be blood.

Johnston testified she believed there was blood on the window curtain in the bathroom, on the bathroom floor, the wall, and the vanity. When she lifted the garbage bag out of the can in the bathroom, she found a bundle of money beneath it.

"And in photograph 52, what do we see to the right-hand side of that radiator?" asked MacKay.

"To the right-hand side there was a skateboard, a bat, and an axe behind the skateboard."

MacKay turned her attention to a photograph of a chair at the kitchen table.

"If you come in the front door, this chair would be immediately to your left," Johnston testified, explaining it also appeared to have been bloodstained.

There were also photographs showing numbered cards, crime-scene markers, to show the location of items the officers seized. There was one on a dresser in the south bedroom, which appeared to belong to William Sandeson.

"There was photo IDs and certificates in the name of William Sandeson," Johnston testified.

MacKay told the court they would watch video showing those items later, and moved on to a photograph of a black backpack with a Canadian flag on it, located inside Sandeson's bedroom.

Johnston testified the backpack contained a black garbage bag in which they found money, mostly twenty-dollar bills, totalling $2,270.

"They appeared to be wet and stained red," she told the jury.

"Okay, did you notice anything else about that bag of money?"

"There was a strong smell coming from the bag."

"What smell?"

"I could best associate it to decomposition."

Johnston continued with a close-up photo of the opened bag.

"On the twenties you can see there's a light red liquid," she said.

"And was it in liquid form then?" asked MacKay.

"Yes."

Johnston then described photos that show her hand holding a Hemastix, which is a presumptive test for blood. She used it on the liquid found in the bag and explained that it did test positive for blood, but that it can also test positive for other substances as well.

"What are you wearing on your hand?" MacKay asked.

"A glove, a nitrile glove," she said, explaining the synthetic gloves police use for handling evidence.

"So did you have gloves on both hands or not, or do you know?"

"Gloves on both hands while I was examining."

"Okay. Throughout the examination of the apartment, were you gloved or not?" asked MacKay, trying to pre-empt what she knew was coming in the cross-examination by the defence.

"When I was photographing and videotaping, I had one glove on for the hand that I would touch something...if I had to open a door. But my hand that I had the camera with didn't have a glove on it. On my feet I had the tyvek booties that go up to your knees. That's what I wore," detailed Johnston, but MacKay didn't stop there.

"And why do you wear gloves and booties?"

"Gloves so that my hand doesn't come in contact with the exhibits and booties so my feet or the bottom of my boots don't come in contact with the staining on the floor."

"Okay, for what reason then?"

"Just to prevent, if there's anything on the bottom of my boots, carrying them into the scene."

"And what about your gloves?"

"The gloves is just to protect my hands from my DNA being left at the scene or from any fluids coming in contact with my hands."

Police also found a Smith & Wesson box in Sandeson's room. Johnston testified it was labelled "William Sandeson P.I.F."

"Are you familiar with guns?"

"A little bit."

"Do you know what P.I.F. might stand for?"

"I don't know what P.I.F. is."

Police say they never did confirm what P.I.F. meant, but an employee of one local gun shop that did not sell William Sandeson his gun, says it likely means "Paid in full" and was probably put there by the seller, not Sandeson. When someone purchases a handgun in Canada, they can't walk out with it the same day. It usually takes five days to receive the legal paperwork transferring the gun into that person's name, so they tag the box while they wait for the new owner to pick it up.

"The gun box, do you know whether there was anything in it?" MacKay asked Johnston.

"No, it was empty," she replied.

Johnston also testified there were two laptops in the room, which were seized, as well as a sword. In the centre of the bedroom, she said, there was a chair with a pair of khaki pants on top of a pile.

"And what condition did the pants appear to you to be?"

"They were in good condition but there was a couple of small stains on the front, and those were seized."

The next photos showed a roll of duct tape, two new hammers with bags over the ends, a knife inside a sheath, and vinyl exam gloves.

And if there were any doubt about whose bedroom in which all of these things were found, Sergeant Sandra Johnston further solidified it when she found a photo ID on the dresser.

"From, I think, Capital Health," she said, using the former name for the now amalgamated Nova Scotia Health Authority.

"Okay, and do you recall whose name it was in?"

"Yes, William Sandeson."

She also found certificates with his name on them and a wallet.

"And did you examine the contents?"

"I think I opened it and saw there was ID identifying William Sandeson."

With the search of the bedroom complete, Johnston moved on to the hallway closet, where she located a series of Mason jars covered in a black garbage bag.

"And what did that appear to be to you?"

"I wasn't sure. There appeared to be something growing inside the Mason jars."

In the same closet, Johnston said she found a Ziploc baggie containing what appeared to be mushrooms.

It seemed every inch of the apartment had been photographed. Johnston was now on photo #109, an image of the kitchen table showing what she described as "white marks" or "wiping patterns" on the top.

"What do you mean by wiping patterns?"

"There appears to be striations. If you look on the right side of the table you can see lines that run parallel to the edge of the table. It almost looks like there was a wiping mark there."

She said the same marks were visible on the front right table leg, and what appeared to be bloodstaining on the table, the chair, and the front door.

Meanwhile, Detective Constable Furlong was searching the dining room area.

"He located what appeared to be a bullet hole in the window frame along the right-hand side," Johnston testified.

It was 10:45 A.M. on August 19.

"Did he draw it to your attention at that time?" Susan MacKay asked Johnston.

"Yes," Johnston replied, testifying she and her partner contacted the sergeant in charge of the force's forensic identification section, and had him attend with a trajectory kit to map the bullet's path.

Sergeant André Habib testified he went to the Henry Street apartment with the trajectory kit. He used photographs from the scene to explain to the jury how he placed a rod in the hole determined to be the bullet's entry point in the window frame. At the end of the rod, he placed a laser.

"Having the laser kit on the end of that trajectory rod allows you to project a spot into space to kind of give you an idea of where that projectile may have come from," he explained.

"Okay, and you're talking about a projectile being a bullet?" MacKay asked.

"Yes," Habib agreed, pointing out that police also placed a fluorescent string along the line projected by the laser to help people visualize the bullet's path.

But the officers didn't just find the hole; when Furlong removed the window casing around the hole, he found the bullet itself in the frame.

Johnston testified she was the one to seize it.

When they returned to the apartment just after 3 p.m., Detective Constable Furlong sprayed the area looking for blood. He did that using a protein staining called Amido Black. It stains the proteins in blood but it's also not a perfect test.

"It's not a presumptive test for blood like the Hemastix was, so it would stain any proteins that are in the blood or other bodily substances," explained Johnston. "You spray it on and then you let it sit for a little bit and then you wash it off with distilled water and the staining remains."

The jury looked at photos of the kitchen after it had been sprayed.

"And what, if anything, did that process indicate to you?"

"There's a possibility it could be bloodstaining in that area," Johnston testified.

With the inside of the apartment examined, the officers headed outside. Johnston took photos of the vacant business to the left, a former laundromat and video store.

"I believe that's Dalhousie property on the right-hand side," she said.

The scene, where William Sandeson lived, was very close to the campus on which he was about to start medical school. The university's Schulich School of Law and Rebecca Cohn Auditorium were one block north of his apartment, a Dalhousie residence one block to the west, and the Dalplex fitness centre just beyond that.

There were also photographs showing the exits and entrances to the apartment. Those would turn out to be critical later in the trial.

"One hundred and fifty-nine is an overall of the exterior view of the window in the northerly bedroom." It was the bedroom that belonged to William Sandeson's roommate.

"Okay. You took this photograph?"

"I did."

"How did you get to that spot?" Susan MacKay asked. That "spot" was a ledge or roof outside the window.

"I crawled through the window," said Johnston.

"You crawled through the window?" repeated MacKay.

"Yes."

The officers left the Henry Street apartment again, but returned one more time later that evening at 8:20 P.M. when they gained access to the code for the safe in Sandeson's bedroom. Inside, they discovered a nine-millimetre handgun with a trigger lock.

"It had a clip in the bottom of it...an empty clip, and to the right of that was a box of, I believe, American Eagle nine-millimetre rounds," said Johnston, still explaining photographs.

"I removed the clip and there was one live round in the clip of the firearm."

She went on to say she and her partner opened the box of ammunition and there were two rounds missing. Johnston also took photos of two jugs of bleach when she went back that evening because she had been told they could be a point of interest.

Detective Constable Furlong brought a reciprocal saw, which he used to remove several portions of the flooring in the kitchen that evening.

"Why was the flooring cut?" MacKay asked.

"It was to see if there was any pooling underneath the flooring."

"Pooling of what?"

"Pooling of possible blood," said Johnston, going on to describe a photo of one of the pieces of flooring.

"It shows the staining had gone down and the protein staining had reacted in the area about two millimetres down in the wood."

Then it was time for show and tell.

One after another, Sergeant Sandra Johnston began producing items she and her partner (who had by now retired) had seized from William Sandeson's apartment, and one after another they were entered as exhibits in his murder trial.

First, the gun.

It wasn't audible but there seemed to be collective awe in the courtroom as those seated in the gallery realized this was the murder weapon, the smoking gun so to speak, that had killed Taylor Samson.

"Did it have any bullets in it?" MacKay asked.

"It did. It had one live round."

"Is the gun, in the condition that it's in right now, is it safe to handle?"

"It is safe to handle, yes, but it was treated with cyanoacrylate, which is a chemical, on the outside, and there was what appeared to be blood on the slide, so that's why I have gloves on."

Johnston testified she was in the lab around 7: 20 A.M. on August 21 when the gun was placed in the cyanoacrylate cabinet.

"It's basically Super Glue, and you heat it up and the vapours adhere to fingerprints on non-porous surfaces," she said.

Officers found some fingerprints and some small, red staining along the gun's slide near the muzzle and at the tip of the muzzle.

"And how big were these...this staining that you noticed?"

"Very small. Under a millimetre."

"All right. And what did it appear to look like to you?"

"It appeared to look like blood."

Johnston also produced the trigger lock—the device that locks over the trigger making it inaccessible—the gun box, the box of bullets, the bullet found inside the gun, the bullet found in the window casing, a piece of the window casing itself, a piece of stained seat cover cut from a chair at the kitchen table, three pieces of stained flooring, the $5,000 found beneath the garbage bag in the bathroom's garbage can, and the stained bathroom window curtain.

Johnston testified she and her partner double-checked each other's work and did a walk-through of the scene with the forensic investigator and the lead investigator before securing the scene.

THE DEFENCE CHALLENGES JOHNSTON

Then it was Brad Sarson's turn to cross-examine her.

He asked Johnston to reiterate why it was important not to contaminate the scene. She agreed that the point of processing a scene is to try and capture things as close to as they were at the time of the alleged crime.

"I'm a little bit curious," Sarson continued. "As I understand it, you can not only wear booties made of Tyvek but there are also entire suits made of Tyvek, is that right?"

"Yes," Johnston agreed.

"And as I understand it, it's kind of like a snowsuit?"

"Yes."

"It includes a hood?"

"Yes."

"All right. What determines whether it's appropriate simply to wear Tyvek booties as you did in this case, or whether it's appropriate to wear an entire suit made of Tyvek?"

"It depends on the scene. If you're in a vehicle, it's a smaller area, you're more likely to come in contact with other surfaces. So I'd be more likely to wear a full suit when I'm in a car. If it was a large bloodletting scene, I would wear the suit."

"Why do you say that for a large bloodletting scene you would wear the suit?"

"When I say 'large' I mean large splashes on the wall or pooling or any potential where I'd have to be in contact with the stains."

"That's one thing I wanted to address with you, Sergeant. As a police officer—as a beginning police officer—I assume that you are taught the importance of taking notes?"

"Yes." It was a question the defence would ask nearly every officer that took the stand.

"That information, which has to be relayed at a much later date, should be recorded very soon after the fact that it's learned so that, when you're in court many many months later, you have something to assist you in refreshing your memory with respect to events of that time period, correct?"

"Yes."

"Okay. In spite of the fact that I would anticipate that that would be sort of one of the first things you'd be taught as an officer, in this case, my understanding is that you did not have any notes. Is that correct?"

"I don't have any notes with me, that's correct."

"Okay. Do you have any handwritten notes at all?"

"I do have handwritten notes."

Sarson asked for a moment in the absence of the jury, before stating neither he nor Eugene Tan were aware that Sergeant Johnston had handwritten notes. There is a general duty on the part of the Crown to disclose all material it proposes to use at trial and especially all evidence, which may assist the accused.[1]

Justice Arnold asked the Crown to step in.

---

1 Director of Public Prosecutions Act.

"Perhaps we can ask Sergeant Johnston about the notes?" asked MacKay. And the trial entered a voir dire.

Voir dires take place in open court but in the absence of the jury, so their contents are protected under a publication ban until the jury is sequestered. Unlike in the United States, Canadian juries are rarely sequestered until they begin deliberating the verdict.

"I've misplaced that notebook," said Johnston.

"Okay. And have you made any computer [notes]?"

Johnston said that when she returned to the police station just after noon on August 19 she wrote notes in Versadex, an internal database used by police. The Versadex file had already been disclosed to the Crown and hence to the defence.

"Any other handwritten notes?" Susan MacKay asked.

"No. After this file happened, I was finishing off my time in Ident and I had just been promoted, and I packed up my desk of ten years and I don't know where the notebook is. I've looked everywhere for it."

"Okay. So what was entered into Versadex?"

"What I did at the scene. And Detective Constable Furlong was with me the entire day from the time we arrived at 5:45 A.M., and it would have been the same timeline that he has in his notebook that I have."

"Okay. And what do you recall about how much your Versadex notes reflected what was in your handwritten notes, and can you tell the court whether or not your Versadex notes were lengthier or shorter than your handwritten notes?"

"My Versadex notes are usually much longer than my handwritten notes. My handwritten notes have my comings and goings and usually a small drawing of the scene."

"Okay, thank you."

But it wasn't enough for Brad Sarson.

"Just so we're clear, you did take handwritten notes, correct?" he asked, still in the absence of the jury.

"I did," Johnston replied.

Sarson continued, asking the specific times Johnston would have made those handwritten notes, but she could not recall.

"Had you ever disclosed to the Crown that you couldn't find your notebook?"

"Yes."

"Okay. And when did you disclose that to the Crown?"

"Last week. I continued searching until last week."

Sarson also wanted to know how long the notebook had been missing but Johnston couldn't recall that either.

"And what efforts have you made to try and locate that notebook since that time?"

"I went through my entire locker. I went through—I have a drawer in the office, went through that. And I have gone through my house. I've gone through pockets, I've looked extensively."

Sergeant Johnston was asked to step outside.

"M'lord, defence obviously caught by surprise by Sergeant Johnston's testimony with respect to a lost notebook," Brad Sarson began his argument, still in the absence of the jury.

"Let me stop you there," Justice Joshua Arnold cut in. "Had you received any of her handwritten notes by way of disclosure at any time?"

Sarson and Tan agreed they had never received any handwritten notes from Johnston, but Arnold challenged them, pointing out that if they had never had any notes and they still didn't have any notes they shouldn't be surprised. He was tough on both the defence and the Crown throughout the trial. But Sarson didn't back down. He argued the issue was that the notes had been lost and that the Crown was aware and did not disclose the matter.

Susan MacKay said she had only known for a week and with a lot of things going on in relation to trial prep she had simply forgotten to tell the defence. The defence was eventually satisfied and agreed to proceed after further investigation into Halifax Police electronic note taking and how it corresponds to the handwritten notes.

At this point, the judge pointed out that six days into the trial not a lot had been accomplished.

"The ongoing issue that we've had so far is that we have a jury of fourteen people who are involved in this case and are not really being able to participate yet at this stage," Justice Arnold told the lawyers, asking if they were confident they would be able to complete the trial in the thirty-two court days that had been set aside. The trial didn't sit on Fridays. The lawyers agreed they were on track.

Constable Alicia Joseph told the court she went to William Sandeson's apartment shortly after 6 P.M. on August 18. She said she was told she was entering the apartment under exigent circumstances under the preservation of life. She went into the bathroom, looked around and looked behind the door. She was looking for Taylor Samson.

"I remember noting that the bathroom was kind of grimy, not well kept, but I remember thinking, the bathtub's spotless and there's no shower curtain. I thought that was kind of odd."

On cross-examination she testified she didn't notice any signs of foul play in the apartment.

Detective Constable Jason Shannon testified he was on his way to Truro on the evening of August 18. He had been asked to go there to look for a vehicle, but he didn't get far. He got a call from the lead investigator informing him William Sandeson had been located at an address on Leaman Drive in Dartmouth. He went there instead to assist other officers in making the arrest. It was around 8 P.M.

"As I was pulling up there, Mr. Sandeson was exiting the residence there, and by the time I got turned around he was already under arrest."

As Sandeson was taken away, he left behind a backpack, which Shannon seized. It was a black Dal Track and Field bag. Shannon produced the contents for the jury. Inside a Winners bag there was a bath mat and a shower curtain, along with a receipt dated

August 18. The items were entered into evidence one by one: a protein shaker, protein, an iPhone charger, black gloves, a wallet, a Dodge Ram decal, Axe body spray, a VISA card in the name of Sonja Gashus, and $66 in Canadian currency. Finally, Shannon handed over the empty backpack to also be entered in evidence.

On cross-examination, defence began by asking Shannon if he knew the importance of taking notes, whether he did take notes, and what he was wearing. Shannon did not take notes because he was just assisting and also didn't realize the case would "balloon." He testified he was not wearing gloves or a so-called "bunny suit" typically worn by forensics officers. He was not asked why and did not offer an explanation.

He also testified he did not see any signs of foul play.

Next up was Detective Constable Roger Sayer, now lead investigator in the Samson homicide, although he wasn't at the time the murder occurred. He began by telling the court he had been a police officer for fifteen years, including seven years on general patrol before becoming a detective in the Criminal Investigation Division. He worked in the drug unit for a brief time before transferring to the General Investigation Section, handling break and enters, robberies, arson, that sort of thing. Following that he worked in the sexual assault unit for four months before he was transferred to homicide, where he had been for four and a half years. In short, Sayer had pretty much done it all.

He told the jury he was called on August 17, 2015, to assist with a missing persons file. It was deemed to be of concern because of a pre-existing medical condition and because police had information a large drug transaction was occurring at the time of the disappearance. He was asked to be a part of what police call the investigative triangle. His first role was as file coordinator, the officer charged with preparing and issuing tasks to other investigators as well as preparing documents that would be put in the file. The other members of the triangle were Detective Constable Kim Robinson, who was then the lead investigator, and Sergeant Derrick Boyd, team leader. As he sat directly addressing the jury, Sayer explained that Boyd's role as team leader was to obtain resources. Robinson, he said, was responsible for the flow and direction of the case. Robinson was promoted to sergeant two months later, at which time Sayer took over as lead investigator.

AFTER THE ARREST

Sayer said he was the first to interview William Sandeson following his arrest on August 18, 2015, and into the early morning hours of August 19. This interview took place before Corporal Jody Allison arrived and the two started their good cop/bad cop charade, and before Sandeson started talking about Morphsuited intruders bursting into his apartment to kill Taylor Samson.

Sayer told the court Sandeson was polite, very quiet, and calm, appearing to be paying attention to everything that was being put to him. The Crown then began playing the video of Sandeson being interviewed for the jury.

When the video begins it is 9:41 P.M. on August 18. Sandeson is in the interrogation room alone. There are two chairs in the room, but they are both empty. He's lying on the floor on his stomach, face down. Within a couple of minutes, Constable Jason Shannon enters the room, takes Sandeson's particulars, and tells him he's under arrest for kidnapping, trafficking, and misleading the police. He was never actually charged with those offences.

William Sandeson remains calm as Constable Shannon reads him his rights and asks if he wishes to call a lawyer. He says "yes." The two leave together at 9:47 P.M. and come back at 10:20 P.M.

In the video Sandeson is again alone, his head in his hands.

Detective Constable Sayer enters the room at 10:27 P.M. Only short snippets of the conversation were played for the jury, the remainder having been deemed inadmissible. The judge told the jury they should not guess or speculate about what had been removed or why.

The publication ban on that material has now been lifted.

The interview shows Sandeson in that same empty interrogation room.

"I want you to know, William, I've been part of this investigation from the beginning. I'm one of the officers that's taking the lead in this investigation," Sayer begins. "I had an opportunity to see almost everything that was done in relation to this investigation and I've been doing this stuff for a long time, William."

Sandeson sits, nodding as Sayer explains that many officers are working on the case putting together the pieces of the puzzle.

"I'm a firm believer, William, that people make choices in their life, and when they do sometimes they're good choices and sometimes they're bad. Does that mean that good people can make bad choices? Yeah, it can."

Sandeson remains silent.

"After putting all these pieces of the puzzle together, there's no doubt in my mind that you were involved in what happened to Taylor. There's no doubt."

Sayer explains that he doesn't think Sandeson is evil like many of the people he sees in this room. Using a sports analogy, he references the Toronto Blue Jays's improbable winning streak in 2015, explaining no one player can do it all, but rather they each have a role on the team.

"You have a role in this file," he tells Sandeson. "What I don't know is how deep your role is."

As it would again and again in this case, the conversation returns to William Sandeson's chosen profession.

"If you want to be a doctor, there's some part of you that wants to do some good in this world."

Sayer has printouts of Sandeson's texts with Samson in his hand.

"I know what was on your phone," he tells Sandeson. "And you know I know. So I need to know where he is." Sayer pauses. "You know where he is, Will."

Sandeson shakes his head. "I don't know," he barely whispers.

"Or you know what happened," Sayer continues.

"I don't know," Sandeson mumbles, his hands clasped together at his mouth.

"I understand that you're scared. I get that. People do things for certain reasons and fear is one of them, but you have to understand that there's a man's life at stake."

Sayer may or may not have known it was too late for Taylor Samson.

"You're a young man, you can move forward from this. But it starts now. This is the biggest day of your life moving forward and you need to make a choice of what you're going to do."

Sayer is all but pleading for answers, speaking in a gentle, coaxing manner.

"What are you going to do, Will? Are you going to let that family suffer? Are you going to let that mom grow old with a broken heart? Never knowing what happened to her son, over some weed? Is that who you're going to be? Are you a monster?"

But it is of no use. Sandeson continues to exercise his right to silence.

"How does a guy go from being a student athlete, going to university, wanting to be a doctor, to not giving a shit about leading a man possibly to his death? How does that happen?"

This is the stuff the judge did not want the jury to hear.

"You haven't even been willing to tell me if I'm being a fool in thinking I could still help this man."

Eventually at 2:07 A.M., Sandeson is taken to police cells, where he is provided a bed and food.

⌐ ⚕ ☘

The next morning at 9:50 A.M., the RCMP's then Constable Jody Allison took over the questioning. (In Halifax, local police and the RCMP operate as an integrated unit.) Sayer told the court Sandeson was very upset during that interview, crying, sobbing, at times finding it difficult to breathe. That stopped later that evening when Sayer returned to question Sandeson once again. He told the court

Sandeson stopped crying and again appeared to be listening very intently.

Sayer said he used two different approaches when interviewing Sandeson on the 18th and the 19th. On the 18th, he used an emotional approach, mentioning family and appealing to Sandeson's desire to help people. "It's a calmer approach," said Sayer.

"The second night when you see me go in, I take a firmer direct approach and I'm factual and I'm talking about evidence." This is when he played the role of bad cop.

Sayer explained that while police did get a search warrant to enter Sandeson's apartment, they didn't wait for it to be produced, citing what police call exigent circumstances, meaning time was of the essence. Sayer explained that to have the warrant written, produced, and executed took nearly ten hours and at the time police believed they might still be able to save Taylor Samson's life. Police didn't actually seize items until they received the warrant around 5:30 A.M. on August 19.

One of the items seized was a DVR, or digital video recorder. With Sayer on the stand, the court played video for the jury showing the hallway outside William Sandeson's apartment between 10:19 and 10:41 on the evening of Saturday, August 15. Sayer walked the jury through what they were seeing as Sandeson came and went. This is the video Sandeson told police had recorded over itself every twenty minutes. He was either lying or, more likely, didn't understand how his own equipment worked.

Sayer told the jury the first thing they should notice was Sandeson going downstairs to the entrance of the apartment building around 10:20. He comes back with two other young men, whom he escorts to his friend Pookiel McCabe's apartment across the hall from his own. The two individuals are only there for two or three minutes before they leave the same way they arrived.

Sayer told the jury this was important because the time frame corresponds with a text message on Sandeson's phone when he told Samson, "Actually hold dude bunch of traffic."

At 10:26, the video shows Sandeson going downstairs again. This time he comes back up with Taylor Samson. Samson is carrying a large black duffle bag. The two enter Sandeson's apartment. Sayer pointed out that the time stamp corresponds with text messages between the two, "I'm out back" and "I'm on my way down."

Next, Sayer told the jury to notice Sandeson's apartment door opening. The video shows a shoulder in the jacket Sandeson was seen wearing a few minutes prior. The door is only open for a couple of seconds and then it closes.

At 10:30, the door opens again. Sandeson goes across the hall. The two people in that apartment enter the hallway looking inside Sandeson's residence. They would become the trial's star witnesses.

At 10:40 Sandeson steps out, not wearing a shirt now, and places something in a shoe rack that you can see in the hallway. He goes back inside. You later see another man arrive at the apartment and pick up the item. It is not clear in the video, but later testimony indicated that the item was marijuana, which means Sandeson effectively did a drug deal in the midst of the murder, or at least the cleanup.

The Crown skipped ahead to the next morning. It's 5:52 A.M. on Sunday, August 16, 2015. William Sandeson is seen leaving his apartment, with his girlfriend, Sonja Gashus. He's wearing a sweater and a bright orange toque. At 6:05 A.M. Sandeson returns to his apartment. The jury later heard he drove his girlfriend and her co-worker to work at a Starbucks in downtown Halifax.

Sandeson leaves again three minutes later. At 9:38 A.M., he returns, now wearing a white tank top, having shed the toque and sweater. A minute later, he leaves again carrying a green compost bin and a spray can. He takes the materials back inside four minutes later along with a large black bag.

The video switched to a different camera. This one shows the exterior of the building. At 9:41, Sandeson gets out of his car, a black Mazda Protegé, and heads for the trunk, taking some items out, and placing others inside.

In court, the Crown moved ahead to Monday, August 17, at 7:52 A.M. Sandeson then leaves his residence wearing a black Dalhousie University backpack and carrying a large KitchenAid box with a grocery bag on top.

Sayer explained that the items shown are important because they were seized when police executed a warrant at an address on Chestnut Street four days later. Inside, officers found the twenty pounds of marijuana believed to have fuelled this crime. (It was the apartment where William Sandeson's younger brother, Adam, lived with his roommates.)

There was one more video.

On Tuesday, August 18, at 8:09 A.M. Sandeson puts some items in the trunk of his car, leaves with the trunk still open, and comes back again two minutes later to put more items in the trunk. They include black garbage bags and a blue Adidas bag. He's wearing bright reddish-orange gloves.

The video complete, Susan MacKay had one more question for Sayer.

"Is this or is this not still an active investigation today?"

"It is," Sayer replied.

"Why?"

"The remains of Mr. Samson have never been located."

"Thank you. Those are my questions for you."

Brad Sarson handled the cross-examination of Detective Constable Sayer for the defence. He began by getting Sayer to reiterate his role in the case, pointing out that information was already coming in, as Samson had been reported missing nearly twenty-four hours prior to Sayer's involvement.

Sayer agreed.

"In a missing persons file what happens, and did happen in this matter, is that family and friends are quite concerned about why their loved one is gone missing, so there is a heavy flow of information coming in of friends, contacts, anywhere they could be. So when you first begin your investigation it's like a large net you throw out because when you have a missing person time is of the essence. So if you want a positive result you have to have it quickly.

"You've made reference to that, or said that a couple of times," said Sarson, "that in a missing person file that time is of the essence. Isn't it fair to say that time is of the essence only if foul play is involved?"

"No, not always," Sayer disagreed. "Because you don't know what could have occurred with a person because we have had people who have gone missing and have been injured, of nobody's design, just has happened, have been attempting to take their own lives, so time is of the essence if you're hoping to find someone and have a positive result when it comes to missing persons."

Sarson also asked Sayer about how Sandeson went from a "person of interest" to a suspect and how and why police began surveillance on him. Sayer testified it was Sergeant Derrick Boyd, who while keeping an eye on Sandeson's first interview, noticed that something wasn't right. As police began obtaining Sandeson's text messages, Boyd picked up on the fact Sandeson hadn't mentioned Samson messaging, "I'm out back of the building now. Is that your bike parked by the door?" But rather he'd told police Samson didn't show up.

Sarson asked when police felt they had reasonable and probable grounds to arrest Sandeson. Sayer explained that during Sandeson's interview with Jody Allison, Sandeson had said Samson was shot in the back of the head. At that time, evidence against Sandeson was already stacking up, and police had found no evidence anyone else had entered the apartment.

"Myself and Sergeant Boyd were watching the video and we looked at each other and we were like, 'His jeopardy's changed.' And we determined it was time to arrest him for murder."

"Even though the information he provided was that someone else had shot Mr. Samson, you and Sergeant Boyd agreed that at that point in time, Mr. Sandeson was arrestable for the murder of Mr. Samson?" asked Sarson.

"We did."

Sarson also asked Sayer about what he knew about Samson's liver disease, asking him to recount the information provided to police by a pharmacist, Samson's mother, and girlfriend in that regard. There had been conflicting information provided about the medical condition at various times. His mother first said he would be okay without his medication for three or four days. She later told police he would be okay for five or six days. Samson's girlfriend, on the other hand, thought he would have to be without his meds for a year in order for it to have a serious impact. Sayer said he placed more weight on Linda Boutilier's testimony because he believed she would be more familiar with his health than a girl he had dated for only a few months.

Sarson pointed out that Samson had been away at university in Halifax for four years and his mother lived in Amherst.

"I would agree with that, sir," Sayer said to Sarson, "but where his mom resided and how many years he had in university would not change his health condition."

"Except you're not a doctor, correct?" Sarson countered.

"No, but I don't think living in Halifax or Amherst, if you have an autoimmune disorder, is going to change that. That's my opinion."

Sarson continued, asking Sayer about names provided by Samson's mother and stepmother regarding possible people Samson was supposed to meet with the night he went missing.

"The evidence led us in a certain direction," Sayer testified. "You put your resources into that direction and you come back if that proves to be not the right direction to go in."

Sarson also asked about attempts to identify the socially awkward man named "Devon" who Samson's girlfriend told police had arrived with a black duffle bag matching the one Samson was last seen carrying. Police spoke with two individuals named Devon but they could not be linked to the person Mackenzie Ruthven described. Sayer said police did not make further attempts to identify the Devon she referenced.

"We already knew that Mr. Samson was at Mr. Sandeson's residence and that's the last place we could put him. And the evidence that police gathered continued to come in after that in that same direction."

Sarson reiterated that Sandeson was charged with murder around 6:45 P.M on August 19.

"I'm going to suggest to you, detective constable, that from that point forward all of the police efforts were dedicated to locating and obtaining evidence in an effort to prove that charge against Mr. Sandeson. Would you agree or disagree?"

"I would disagree, sir. You go where the evidence goes. However, our first concern has always been trying to find Mr. Samson. And so even when Mr. Sandeson had been arrested for his murder and Mr. Samson's remains had not been found, our first priority in the evidence that we were gathering was trying to locate him."

PSYCHIC REPORTS BODY

Sarson asked Sayer about reported sightings of Samson.

"There were tips coming in from the time that the media release was made of Mr. Samson being missing and they have continued today," Sarson said on May 8, 2017, at which time Samson's body still hadn't been found. "Also, since then we've received reports on body location, even psychic reports on people that had feelings of certain areas we should look or check and things like that."

One of those letters was admitted as an exhibit in the case.

Saturday, August 22, 2015
To whomever it may concern,

I am writing to you regarding the case of Taylor Samson. I did not know him personally nor was I aware of who he was until he was reported missing.

Two or three days after his disappearance I was on my way to the supermarket and came across a notice on a telephone poll [sic] advertising his disappearance. I seldom look at ads stapled about the city. However, I happened to look in the direction of this one and it instantly grabbed my attention. I starred [sic] at his picture and read the information on the paper. After having looked at it for only a few seconds I knew he was dead.

Later, either before or after the case had been changed to a homicide investigation. (I cannot remember exactly), I had a vision of the Northwest Arm from the perspective of someone standing on the shore of the peninsula. The vision was focussed on a spot in the middle between the Armdale shore and the peninsula. This spot was darker than the rest of the water, implying that this is where his body was. I also had a vision of him lying on his chest, with his face turned to the left, and his left arm above his head with his palm face down.

I have a strong feeling that his body is there and also have felt that his spirit has been around me. He has been interfering with my ability to fall asleep and when I woke up today, I realized that he was urging me to write this to you. I don't know what you make of this kind of information; whether you value it or dismiss it. However, if all else fails, I highly recommend looking in the Northwest Arm.

Regardless, I wish you well in your investigation.

It was perhaps a sign of the public's intense interest in the case. Some members of the public who had no connection to those involved showed up in court to witness the drama first hand. On more than one occasion there was a lineup outside the courtroom. One day a deputy sheriff asked for volunteers to leave because the courtroom was full and immediate family members of Taylor Samson didn't have a seat. Still others followed along as reporters covering the case live tweeted the testimony, many so intrigued they admitted to ignoring work and other responsibilities; the journalists picking up hundreds, some thousands, of followers as the case progressed.

A Facebook group emerged, Taylor Samson: Case Discussion – TRIAL WATCH. Its members seemed to be obsessed with the case, following every word and fuelling speculation of their own.

Reporter Blair Rhodes says it was the mystery of the case that not only maintained the interest but caused it to build throughout the trial. People wanted to know what happened to Taylor Samson. Where was his body? "How could [Sandeson] who appeared squeaky clean and beloved turn out to be a stone-cold killer?" Rhodes quipped.

Rhodes notes that social media reaction also changed as the trial progressed. There was initially a lot of anger, even pushback, from some who wondered why media would even cover the case because it was so preposterous that Sandeson could murder someone.

"At the beginning of the trial, William Sandeson had a lot of friends," says Rhodes. "As the evidence piled up and up and up, I noticed that they got quieter on social media. They sort of backed off."

Rhodes explains that public reaction to crime is different when ordinary people are killed, as opposed to, for example, gang members. When news of Samson's murder broke in August 2015, there was some initial reaction that he was "just another drug dealer" but Rhodes says that changed.

"I think throughout the duration of the trial, you got a better sense of who he was as an individual, and how beloved he was by family and friends."

While interest was sustained throughout the lengthy trial, the morbid fascination hit a peak on the days the trial's star witnesses took the stand.

"The energy in the courtroom was electric," describes Rhodes, who says his phone was vibrating in his hand because he was getting so many retweets and responses on Twitter, as he relayed what was taking place in the courtroom.

"People were just going nuts at that point. They just couldn't believe it. Those of us who were in the press group that were there, we were just going, 'Oh my God, can you believe this?'"

CHAPTER 9
THE CROWN'S CASE: WITNESS TO MURDER

In the summer of 2015, Justin Blades and Pookiel McCabe were enjoying life. McCabe, who also goes by Kahmall, had just graduated from Dalhousie University with a business management degree. He was bartending at the Casino and running day camps at the Dartmouth Sportsplex. Blades had been pursuing an arts degree, but had dropped out because he didn't have enough money to finish. Both were members of the Dal Track and Field team.

"Always track, every day," Blades would tell a jury nearly two years later.

The team's website shows in 2018 that Blades was still the team record holder in the 400 metres, having run 48.76 in 2012. The team record for the 4 x 400 relay team is still owned by Blades, his friend McCabe, Andrew Falkenham, and Jacob Moore, also set in 2012.

On August 15, the two teammates were anticipating a good night. Blades was at home waiting for McCabe to get ready. "He takes forever, so eventually I got fed up. I don't have a phone that texts so I messaged him on Wi-Fi, through

Facebook or whatever. I have no patience, so he didn't text me back quick enough so I just took off down to the house."

Justin Blades was twenty-six years old at the time he testified in May 2017. Like many of the others whose lives had been turned upside down by the case, he was young and fit. With short brown hair and closely trimmed facial hair, he stood six foot one. He wore a dark grey Roots hoodie to court, where he testified he grew up in Yarmouth, in Southwestern Nova Scotia. It was clear he didn't have an easy life, his upbringing entirely different than the friend against whom he was testifying.

Pookiel McCabe was twenty-four at the time of the trial. McCabe is from Brampton, Ontario. He's six foot three with short black hair and neatly trimmed facial hair. He wore a collared shirt to court.

When Blades arrived at 1210 Henry Street, apartment #1, it was 9:55 P.M. McCabe and William Sandeson, his neighbour from across the hall, were already drinking, smoking weed, and playing video games. The music was a little loud, but not so loud they couldn't have a conversation over it. Blades and McCabe were getting ready for a track and field party. Sandeson had just arrived moments before Blades.

"He came over and we asked if he wanted to come out," McCabe testified. "He didn't want to come out with us." Sandeson left fifteen minutes after Blades arrived.

Blades had had three quarters of a bottle of red wine by the time he arrived. Pookiel McCabe was just getting started. "He usually is a late starter," Blades told the jury. "Course when I got there, I'm gonna rev him up to get in the zone, party."

Blades and McCabe continued alone for a while until Blades got a text from a friend named Adrian asking for some weed. He told him to come and get it. Adrian and his friend, not known to McCabe or Blades, arrived at McCabe's apartment at 10:21 P.M.

"He picked up a gram of weed, wasn't there long. He didn't pay for it, I just gave it to him whatever, it's only weed."

Surveillance video shows the boys leaving just three minutes after they arrive. Two minutes after that, unbeknownst to McCabe and Blades, William Sandeson enters his apartment followed by Taylor Samson. Just three minutes later the evening starts spinning out of control.

"It wasn't long and then we heard a loud bang, real loud," said Blades.

"We didn't know what it was," said McCabe. "We just looked at each other, like, 'What was that?'"

"We were ready to jump out the window," said Blades.

Instead, the two froze for a moment, then jumped up, ran to the door, and locked it.

"Put my head against the door frame, not directly against the door, just to listen," said Blades.

"Didn't hear really anything, just like a little small scuffle, like a table or chair moved." The noise was very quick. We listened, it was quiet and then we heard his door open."

Then there was a knock on their door.

"He said, 'Hey, it's Will,'" Blades recalled. "We didn't open the door, we just waited a second, and he said, 'It's Will. It's okay, open the door.' So I unlocked the door and opened it."

"He seemed like a little shocked, I dunno," said McCabe.

"There he was just standing there," said Blades. "Quick as I opened the door, he turned around and went back into his apartment. He didn't say anything to us."

He said Sandeson was at the door less than a minute after they heard the loud bang. When he left, they followed him across the hall.

"I went first and Kahmall was right behind me. As soon as you went through the door you could just see the scene."

THE ORIGINAL STORIES

But four days after their shocking experience, when police first questioned them, Justin Blades and Pookiel McCabe told officers they saw nothing at all. What would cause them to eventually change their stories was an unpredictable series of events.

Pookiel McCabe was questioned first, on August 19, 2015, at Halifax Police Headquarters, days after Taylor Samson vanished. It was just before five o'clock in the evening. Detective Constable Jonathan Jefferies explained that police were investigating the disappearance of Taylor Samson and had some questions for him. By now the police had secured McCabe's apartment and he couldn't get back in.

He tells police he has been living in apartment #1 alone for two years and that Will Sandeson and Dylan Zinck-Selig live together, across the hall in apartment #2. They've only been there for a year.

The interview shows McCabe withholding information.

"Do you know Taylor Samson?" Detective Constable Jefferies asks.

"No, I don't," says McCabe.

"You don't?"

"No."

"Have you heard about his disappearance?"

"I've heard, I've seen like, on Facebook and stuff like that, yeah."

"All right. Have you heard anything about it through the grapevine or through friends or have you talked about it with anybody or anything like that? "

"No."

McCabe insists repeatedly that he doesn't know Samson at all. About that much at least, he is telling the truth.

"I got off work at 5:30, took the bus home, went upstairs to my room," he continues when Officer Jefferies asks him about the previous evening, August 18.

"And then, like ten minutes after I got in the door, I hear, like, cruisers or whatever come up. So I looked out the window and there's like a bunch of cops down there. And I was like, 'Holy shit, what's going on?'"

He tells Jefferies he was kind of nervous.

"They just, like, ran up to the door, knocked on the door, said, 'Police, police.' So I was like, 'Shit.' Opened the door and I was like, 'What's going on?' And then they just, they didn't really tell me what was happening. They came into my house, asked me some questions, took my name and stuff like that, checked my apartment, said they were looking for a body and they didn't, like I didn't understand that."

"Okay."

"But like, yeah, I let them walk around my house or whatever, and then like, my door was open still and they just kicked down the next door, like next-door neighbour's door."

McCabe says he asked the officers if he could close his door and they told him he could, but he decided he couldn't stay there.

"My heart's just jumping," he tells Jefferies. "Like, what's going on? And they don't want to answer anything."

He takes the officer through everything he had been doing for the past couple of days, just going to work and to the gym, his regular routine.

"So with regards to Will and Dylan, do you know of any criminal stuff that they're into? I mean, you say you know these guys from track."

"Criminal? Like...maybe, like, sell a little weed."

"You know that they sell a little weed?"

"Not Dylan. Will, like, sold a little weed, but like, that's all."

"So when you say a little weed, is it a little or is he doing a lot of business? You know what I mean?"

"Yeah, I don't know. I haven't seen anything out of the ordinary at least."

"All right, so let's go back to the weekend when you're home. Anything out of the ordinary happen when you're home? Did you hear anything?"

This is where McCabe stops telling the truth.

"Like, um, no," he responds.

"No?" asks Jefferies.

McCabe shakes his head.

"So, um, when you were home did you stop over to the neighbour's—"

McCabe cuts him off.

"No, no. I didn't."

"...Will and Dylan's and say hi or anything like that?" Jefferies continues. He knows McCabe went across the hall because he's seen him on surveillance video, but McCabe sticks to his story.

"I didn't stop in, no. I don't think anybody was home."

Jefferies has to be disappointed. He has reason to believe McCabe might have witnessed something crucial.

"Okay, so you never heard anything out of the ordinary?"

"No."

"Never saw anything out of the ordinary?"

"No."

They continue chatting for a few minutes before Jefferies tries one last time. "Anything else you can think of that might have popped in your head the last couple of days that you think I should know?"

"No, it was just that that lawyer called was kind of weird." Sandeson's lawyer had called Pookiel McCabe asking him to go into Sandeson's apartment, get all the cash he could find and bring it to the courthouse. "And ah, yeah, the cops being there," McCabe continues. "Nothing much else."

╭ ℒ ☙

It's a week later before police interview Justin Blades, who had been with McCabe that night. He had gone home to Yarmouth with his girlfriend to visit family.

So police travelled to Yarmouth to question Blades there. It was August 26. The RCMP's Jody Allison (he was still a constable at the time) conducted the interview with Detective Constable Scott MacLeod of Halifax Regional Police. It starts out much the same way as the McCabe interview, with the officers explaining they're investigating the disappearance of Taylor Samson, asking Blades how he knows Sandeson, and what they were doing the previous Saturday night. He tells essentially the same story as his friend, only Blades admits he was talking to Sandeson at his apartment door.

Otherwise, Blades is no more forthcoming than McCabe.

"There was you and Pookiel talking to him at the door?" Allison asks.

"Yeah."

"At his door, his door was open."

"I was still smoking weed, like, pretty much, so..."

"Yeah, do you remember anything out of the ordinary there that you saw?"

"No. Will kept his stuff, like his drug deal stuff, on the down low."

"Okay, did you see anybody in his apartment?"

"No one, not a person," Blades lies, before trying to change the subject.

"All the boys got together after all this and we talked because we're all fucked up from hearing, like..."

But Allison quickly returns to his line of questioning.

"Did you see anything on his table?"

"No, if he had product, like, he wouldn't leave it out, like."

"You're not going to be in trouble for that stuff, like if you saw something, or—"

"No, I will try to help you guys out." He lies again.

Allison reminds Blades he's already spoken to Sandeson and already watched the surveillance video.

"I want you to think about it because it's very important that you tell us the truth."

"Well the only thing I was sketched out about too is when Dylan came in and talked to us...he said he went home and showered and there was no fucking shower curtain."

"Yeah."

"That's just unsettling."

"I don't want you to think that, you know, you had any kind of knowledge about this. That's not what I'm saying. But if you saw something, if the door was open and you saw somebody in there or if you saw something on the table or something like that, then I mean, you know, you're not in trouble for seeing that kind of stuff is what I'm trying to tell you."

"Yeah, like seeing drugs and stuff."

"Yeah," Allison agrees, but it changes nothing.

"Well, I honestly didn't see anything," says Blades, and the police have struck out once again.

The next morning, they try with McCabe again. Allison's handling this one too. This time, McCabe is warned he can be charged for misleading police, but it's no use.

"The door is wide open," Allison is taking McCabe through the sequence of events seen on the surveillance video.

"Yeah," he agrees.

"Right. So there's yourself and Justin standing there."

"Okay."

"Okay? So tell me what you saw."

"I didn't see anything." There it is again. And for fourteen months Justin Blades and Pookiel McCabe maintain their silence.

Then, in October 2016, the two young men were approached by a private investigator, working for William Sandeson's defence team. He wanted to know their stories and for the first time, Blades and McCabe wanted to talk. They told the private investigator everything they knew, and he encouraged them to go to the police, even going so far as to help arrange an interview for Blades. It was a move that almost derailed the case, nearly causing a mistrial.

THE NEW STORIES

On October 20, 2016, the police paid Justin Blades another visit, drove him to police headquarters, and Allison, who had now been promoted to corporal, found himself once again interviewing Justin Blades about that still-mysterious summer night in the South End of Halifax. Both the officer and the witness knew this would be a very different interview.

"It is 12:46 in the afternoon," Allison begins. "And this video is in reference to an investigation by Halifax Regional Police into the homicide of Taylor Samson, okay?"

"Okay," agrees Blades. After more than a year of keeping this terrible secret, he's ready to tell the truth.

"I want you to understand that severe criminal sanctions exist for the making of a false statement," says Sergeant Derrick Boyd, the Commissioner of Oaths. "Do you understand that lying under oath constitutes perjury which may be punished by fourteen years imprisonment?"

"I do. That's heavy."

"Further, do you understand that misleading the police in a criminal investigation is a criminal offence, which may be punishable by five years imprisonment?"

"I do."

"Do you understand that severe criminal sanctions exist for the making of a false statement under oath?"

"I do."

"Is your participation in this statement free and voluntary?"

"Yes, yeah."

Blades affirms the oath, signs the paperwork, and gets down to business with Allison, admitting he didn't tell him the complete truth the first time.

"Okay, and can you explain why you decided to provide police investigators with information regarding this information now?"

"Just never been...tired of being scared."

"And if this were to go to court are you willing to testify under oath as to what you have said here today?"

"I don't know. I don't want to go to court. This has ruined my life enough. I don't need to tarnish everything."

"Okay, Justin, let's talk about what happened that particular time. Let's start earlier in the day. "

Blades's story starts out the same as it did the first time. He was at his friend Pookiel McCabe's getting ready for a track party.

"I show up at Kahmall's like I always do and, yeah, Will is in there and we're all playing video games. And I just remember Will saying he just came back from supper with Sonja and then they said they loved each other for the first time. I remember that really stood out to me."

Blades's friend texts him looking for some weed and two guys come by to get some. They leave at 10:24 P.M. Seconds later, Sandeson leaves too.

"Wasn't long man, like heard the gunshot go off," Blades told Allison. "Both me and Kahmall both stood up and like, being like, *oh fuck, like what the fuck* like, and I ran over and locked the door. I remember that and just being like, *What are we going to do? What do we do? What do we do?* Pretty much, like, fuck, we're going to jump out the window. And I was putting all these scenarios in my head, like, *Oh my God, are we next? Do they know we're over here?* And then we just, like, stood there and stood there like, tried to listen to see if we could hear anything."

"Right."

"And I didn't hear anything, and then we heard the door open and then we were, like, *Oh fuck* and then Will knocked on the door and he was like, I don't remember anything that anyone really said, like, I was so fucking shocked by that point.

"Then I do remember like, the biggest thing that just stuck in my head is just when he opened the door. He opened the door and then his door was open and then as we went to the doorway, like, Will is panicky. He's panicky obviously, like he's going to be panicky, and he's like, running around his apartment with," he trails off. "I guess it was Taylor Samson. You couldn't see who he was because he was slumped over like"—Blades leans forward and bends over—"head down, suffering from a gunshot to the head, blood all over the floor, money all over the place, drugs all over the floor."

"Okay."

"Just like a scene out of a fucking movie, man, like."

"Okay. You mentioned there was drugs, what do you mean when you say, 'drugs'?"

"I seen a bunch of weed but I know they deal more than weed."

"And when you saw it, you could still see, like, the blood pouring down?"

"Yeah, it was still coming out, but there was pints and pints of blood on the floor.

"And we just stood there in the doorway, being like, *What the fuck?* At this point, like, everything's running through my head."

"Do you remember seeing a firearm? Because you heard the shot—"

"No. That's what freaked me out like...like, he wasn't the shooter."

"Okay, now as far as who else was there, anybody else around besides you and Pookie?"

"No, just us three, I guess."

"There wasn't anybody, like you couldn't see anybody in the hallway, down the hallway or anything?"

"No, I only had the doorway image. And I just remember being like, don't even know what I said to him. I didn't even know if I said anything, like, 'What the fuck happened?' pretty much and he just didn't say anything, just running around, like, 'I got to clean this up. I got to clean this up.' And we went back over to the apartment and I was like, 'Kahmall, man, like, we got to call the police. What are we going to do?' And we were just like, 'We'll just go tell him he's got to figure this out. He's going to call the police. We need to get out of here.'"

The two young men glanced inside Sandeson's apartment again.

"And the second time though, like what really fucked me up, is like, when I knock on the door and be like, 'Will, we're leaving,' and like, you could veer in and he moved the body from the position and dragged it into the bathroom. You could see the streaks of blood."

"So you knock on the door the second time, and how far did you, did you go in very far?"

"No, I just stopped at the doorway, no fucking way, man. I wasn't passing there."

"When that happened can you tell me what else you saw in the room at the time? Like anything."

"He was just picking up bloody money."

"Still doing the same thing."

"Yeah."

"I know this is tough, Justin. I just want to make sure we get everything covered off," Allison explains to an obviously emotional Blades. The officer asks him to go through everything again, but this time backwards, explaining that sometimes it helps people remember details they hadn't before, but Blades is struggling to keep it together.

"Justin, listen, you know what, there's people that go through not even a tenth of what you've gone through over this. That guy put you in the position, you didn't get him to do any of this."

"If I wouldn't have been so frigging impatient I wouldn't even have been there. I would have been still at home. Sitting there playing Xbox, waiting for Kahmall to hurry the fuck up. He's always like a girl and he just wants to get pretty."

"But the main thing to remember though is that you didn't do anything wrong. You didn't do anything wrong." The officer tries to console him.

"I did though, I should have at least, I know I feared for my own life, but like, fuck, man, that poor Taylor's mom didn't deserve to look at any of that."

"No," the officer agrees. "The thing is though, you didn't do anything wrong. He did that, he did it, and he brought you into it."

And then that working backwards idea seems to work.

"Even the weirdest part is that he asked me to bring the car around," Blades recalls.

"What? When...when was that?" Allison asks.

"That was the first time he came and got us, and he was like, panicking, and he was just like, throwing shit out of his mouth."

"So did you bring the car around?"

"Fuck, no."

"So what did he mean by that?"

"I don't know."

Only three minutes pass from the time Sandeson first knocks on McCabe's door to the time McCabe and Blades leave the building.

"I was in a panic," Blades tells the police this time. "Like, left everything going, video game is still going, it was just like, 'Will, man, we're leaving. You need to call the fucking police.'"

They headed to Blades's apartment just a short distance away.

"I was sick the whole way, like throwing up and shit, fucking power walking, like didn't know what to do, and then I went in the house and had a poop."

When he came out, Blades says, he and McCabe saw another friend coming up the street, who told them he was on his way to get some weed from Sandeson. He and McCabe didn't warn him or tell him what they had seen. He says the same friend later told them he hadn't gone inside Sandeson's apartment that night because he had left the weed in the hallway for him.

Blades and McCabe carried on to the track and field party as planned because they wanted to be around people. They hung out at the party for a while and then waited for their girlfriends, both bartenders at downtown Halifax nightclubs, to get off work.

"I couldn't wait for her to get off," Blades tells police. When she did, they went to her place for the night.

"I didn't sleep, she slept, and I just laid there, and then at like 10 A.M. in the morning, [she] wanted to go to the beach, and like she knew I was upset, but I didn't tell her why, I just kind of hid it."

He told his girlfriend he wanted to stop at Sandeson's on the way to the beach to get some weed, but it wasn't really about that. He needed to assess the situation, see if he could figure out what had happened and whether the police had been by yet.

"I went inside, knocked on the door, like, I had no idea what the fuck I was going to walk into again."

But to the untrained eye, the apartment was sparkling clean, as though the horrific murder scene had simply vanished.

"He was in his apartment and it just like, smelled like fucking chemicals, and they were so hard. So obviously when I walked in and realized he cleaned the place up, I was in shock again. I was like, *This is not right, this isn't right.*"

His girlfriend was waiting in the car so he didn't stay long.

"I remember just saying like, 'You're supposed to start med school.' I remember like, pep-talking him and being like, 'You're fucked.'"

"Yeah," says Allison. Blades has been talking for a while now. Allison doesn't even have to ask questions this time.

"He says, 'I got this, I'll figure it out. I'll take care of it.'"

But to Justin Blades, it very much appeared that his friend, the aspiring doctor, had already taken care of it, whatever "it" was, he still didn't really know.

"I was scared to come in contact with him because I didn't know what the fuck was going on, so I messaged him on Facebook. I wanted to get him in a public place, where I knew I could talk to him without an environment like that, so I told him I wanted to go kick-boxing with him."

Sandeson said he couldn't go kick-boxing because he was at work.

"And I was like, *What in the fuck is he doing at work?*"

He told Blades he would get in touch the next day and maybe they could go kick-boxing then, but that was August 18, the day Will Sandeson was arrested.

"That's crazy, that's crazy, eh?" says Allison. It's the first time he's spoken in a while.

"Yeah, it's so fucked up, man."

"I mean for him to put you in that position is pretty selfish."

"Oh, if I was left in this room with Will right now, I'd rough him up for sure. I don't know how, like any of the justice system works here, but I almost wanted to go into the jail, and be like, 'I'm tired man, what's going on? You need to come clean, like tell me if I'm being pursued.'"

"That was something you were thinking of doing, you mean?"

"Yeah, stuff like that played in my mind all the time. And then obviously I feel like that was a recording place, like, and then obviously because I didn't tell you guys I could get in trouble."

"So Justin, back around that time, why didn't you tell us that then? What was going on?" asks Allison.

"So the thing is, like, there's hearsay through a lot of people. I knew Will was affiliated with, or whatever, was working for the Hells Angels, and I knew obviously it was a lot of drugs, more than Will is capable of doing with himself."

"Okay."

"You don't fuck with the Hells Angels," says Blades.

"Right. I mean, I can understand that and I can empathize with your position there. This must have been weighing on you for a long time."

"Yeah, I'm so tired of putting a face on the whole time, man, like, fuck. I'm so hurt but I have to hide it."

"Yeah, it's tough and I'll tell you something, you gotta make sure you talk to some people about this when we're done, you know, you make an appointment and talk to the right people, okay? Because something like that, that sticks with a person forever."

"Yeah, I don't know what's going to make it better."

"Justin, by doing what you did right now, you have made some good steps."

"Yeah, poor mom, man, fuck, Taylor's mom, like, obviously I feel for people, I work helping save people's lives." At the time Blades worked in the Emergency Department at Halifax's hospital. "I see a family come in to see their hurt loved ones, and I've been to so many funerals in my family."

"Yeah, so if you could do something to help his mother."

"It's obviously why I'm here."

"That's the reason you're in here," Allison repeats.

"As long as my name doesn't come up in all this shit," Blades says.

"I can tell you right now that if you're concerned about the Hells Angels that he has no connection to the Hells Angels."

"I want to believe you."

"I can tell you that whatever he was telling people, or whatever people believe, I can tell you that is not the case," Allison tells him. "There is no connection. If there was, they would have come after his family for the money and all that. They could have got him in jail if they wanted to."

"Yeah," is all Blades can offer.

"I'm not saying that some of the stuff that he didn't buy somehow made it to them, or some of the money didn't, but I can tell you right now that the stuff he had, you can get from people that have no affiliation to the Hells Angels right here in this city."

"Just basically people are growing in their basements," says Blades.

"Right," agrees Allison. "They wouldn't deal with him anyway, you know what I mean."

"I just heard because he was fucking, like they needed someone smart like Will, like it just made so much sense when you looked at it."

"They usually look for dummies," Allison says.

Stephen Schneider has been researching organized crime in Canada since the late 1980s. He teaches it at Saint Mary's University and he's written three books on the subject, including *Iced: The Story of Organized Crime in Canada*. He says historically it was true that the Hells Angels weren't necessarily looking for intelligence but that times have changed.

"They wanted people to kind of fit their stereotype—big, tough-looking, intimidating—but increasingly they are looking for smart people because they're moving away from the kind of knuckle-dragging biker group and they're now more of a sophisticated well-oiled criminal machine," he explains.

It seems many of the rumours that William Sandeson was involved with organized crime were fuelled by Sandeson himself. Blades tells police Sandeson had told him a story about going to Montreal to do a deal with the Hells Angels.

"I can tell you that they wouldn't be dealing with him," Allison reaffirms. "I can guarantee they would not."

"If he was dealing with the Hells Angels, he wouldn't have gone necessarily to Montreal," says Schneider in our interview. "He would have gone to Ontario because Halifax and Nova Scotia was being controlled by the Gatekeepers [an affiliate club] out of London, Ontario." He points out while the Angels are well represented in Quebec, they deal mostly in hash and cocaine there, not marijuana.

Schneider also says the Angels have distanced themselves from street-level trafficking because it simply isn't profitable.

"They tend to be more just involved with financing of grow ops, things like that, and most of the marijuana trafficking that the Hells Angels do is exported to the United States. They don't do a lot of trafficking in Canada, because they get bigger money in the US, double what they would make here."

The gossip also seems to have grown from the average citizen's understanding of drug deals.

"A patched Hells Angel member's not going to deal in twenty pounds of weed," Corporal Allison tells Justin Blades back in the fall of 2016, "not even a hundred pounds of weed. If you're bringing in maybe fifty keys [kilograms] of coke, they wouldn't even touch it themselves."

"It's not worth it for them?" Blades asks the officer, seeking reassurance.

"It's not worth it for them," Allison confirms. "Plus they don't want to go to jail."

Stephen Schneider agrees. "The Hells Angels, when they do deal in pot, deal in tonnes, not pounds," he says. "If you had twenty pounds of heroin or fentanyl or cocaine, then yeah, that's huge, but not marijuana."

Schneider says the Angels have learned from the past and would now have three to four intermediaries between them and a street-level dealer.

"They would be so far removed that generally speaking I can't see any full-patch member of the Hells Angels in Quebec or Ontario having a relationship with this guy."

"There is nothing that we have found in any part of this investigation that would lead us to think that there's anybody from the Hells Angels or any other criminal organization that's interested in him," Allison tells Blades.

"So stupid," Blades mutters. "I don't know why I deserve to even—"

Allison interrupts him. "No, you don't want to think like that. You don't want to think like that at all. You didn't go and put yourself in this situation. This is the other guy. For whatever reason, who knows why he did it, he pulled you and your friend into it. He ruined—"

"Ruined Kahmall's life," Blades interjects. "Like, fuck, he's not the same, and he was my best friend, too. We just can't even look at each other the same."

"So, Pookiel, he saw everything that you pretty well saw, did he?"

"Yeah, he was with me there."

"He was right beside you."

"Yeah."

┏ 🩺 🌿

Days later, Nova Scotia police travelled to Ontario and surprised Pookiel McCabe early one morning as he was getting ready for work. He agreed to go with them to a local detachment for the third time. Like his friend Justin Blades, this time, McCabe also told the truth and the two would go on to testify at William Sandeson's trial in the spring of 2017. McCabe's story was not as detailed or dramatic as Blades's, but the facts were the same.

"We just like walked across the hall and looked in his apartment and saw a man there sitting in a chair. He had blood on him. Me and Justin looked in there. We didn't look that long."

McCabe could not back up Blades's account of Sandeson running around in a panic, cleaning up bloody money.

"I wasn't focused on him. I was just like in shock."

Like Blades, McCabe also cited fear as the reason he didn't tell the truth for more than a year.

"I didn't know if he was affiliated with anybody, like if he was affiliated to any organized crime or something," he told the jury.

Also like Justin Blades, Pookiel McCabe saw William Sandeson after he witnessed the horrific scene in his apartment, but the circumstances were different. McCabe went home later that night. He admitted he was intoxicated.

"When I got there I had received a text message from William. He just wanted to know if I was still up. I said 'yes' and he came over and like, we just played video games."

Surveillance video shows Sandeson enter McCabe's apartment at four o'clock in the morning, and for an hour and a half the two played *Call of Duty* and listened to SoundCloud, an online music-sharing platform.

"Did you talk about anything?" asked Crown Attorney Susan MacKay.

"We didn't," said McCabe in court.

"Did you talk about the things that you had seen in his apartment?"

"Honestly, I didn't want to bring it up."

"And how did that feel to you? That interaction with him at that time?"

"From what I can remember it was a weird feeling."

CONTACT WITH SANDESON

At 5:28 A.M., Sandeson went home, but it would not be the last interaction between him and McCabe. They continued corresponding with Sandeson behind bars.

"He wrote letters to me," McCabe told the jury.

Sandeson's letters were not introduced as evidence, but McCabe's responses were.

Ay homie, he wrote in a typed letter in November 2015, three months after Sandeson was arrested for murder.

I would never chuck out your letter without reading it or replying. I just hope you're staying strong and safe, so I'm happy that I did get your letter, and that you've got some people you're cool with keeping you fed. Yes, and I've talked to Sonja, she says she speaks to you frequently now, that's awesome. She cares about you a lot man. But $20 for 7 minutes? They don't have any better phone plans than that?! No discounts?!? Ya leave it to Andrew to snag your liquor, using it to wine and dine Bianca, no doubt. We'll definitely get some shots of Glen Fiddich when all is said and done. You're right, fuzz and media had been annoying trying to talk to basically anyone you came into contact with. I wish you the best of luck in finding someone else to represent you, if that's still your goal.

I'm still holding it down part-time at the Casino. Now that I'm out of school I get so bored, it sucks, and sometimes I don't know what to do with myself all day. Lol See, I make enough to get by part-time and really don't want to work a lame full-time job because I want enough time to work on music and DIEM. *So I've decided I'm going to focus on those two things, music and the brand, and just go super hard. Frequent songs, covers and new designs and start monetizing. That's what I want to do with my life, make good music and make some cool clothes! I've got some sweet jams coming out before the years end, I've stepped my production and mixing game up nice. When you get to the booth I'll have a nice beat library for you to choose from, you can finally lay your bars down.*

Something I've recently started to read up on with my free time was investing and the stock market, it finally peaked my interest when I read the book 'Rich Dad Poor Dad' by Robert Kiyosaki. I think I remember you talking about getting into it? but I didn't know much about stocks or how they worked. So when I do start pulling in some extra cash, I'll be looking to start investing.

Emily and I are good, I've been spending a lot of time at her place recently and I'll be going to St. John. NL [sic] *to visit her sister's new place and have Christmas there. I also think they have plans to get me screeched in, that's a big step.*

Keep up your routine and write me anytime mang. keep me posted on your case too if you want/can. I neglect my phone because the sim card's still fucked and I'm cheap. (I use it mainly for wi-fi) But you don't have a good phone plan available so it doesn't matter. :P

The crew misses you and we'll always be here for you.

Keep your head up, Guillermo. [He closed the letter with the Spanish term for "William."]

"You have to understand that me and Will had known each other for five years," McCabe told the jury. "So we had grown really close, and like our whole team, we had a group of friends, he was part of our group of friends so I just wanted to let him know that there was other people that missed him."

Just over a year later in January 2016, McCabe responded to another letter from Sandeson. Again, it's not known what Sandeson wrote, but we can gauge some of the conversation by McCabe's response

Waddup cuz, he wrote, this time in a handwritten letter.

I hope you made the most of your Christmas and have a Happy New Year! And that 2016 will bring some new tunes to the radio so that you're not being brainwashed by all of its repetitive songs.

Hah Also, I looked up that A-K *rapper you told me about, he's pretty good. lol he is a very animated sounding gangsta rapper.*

St. Johns weather isn't bad at the moment, it had one snowfall but it quickly melted the next day when it hit 6°C. I visited Signal Hill, then Cape Spear, the most eastern point in Canada and I hit up a couple breweries. I also saw Chantal Gordon over there at Costco. I had plans to get screeched in one night, but Emily, her sister Olivia, Olivia's boyfriend and I all got way too drunk the night before, so we put it off for another couple of days to recover (or keep it at a nice social buzz.) The day we were all ready to get me screeched in we called the place with the best Screech in and they said they weren't doing them again until the New Year. That night we went to George St. and the streets were dead! A few people in the six or so bars that were open. So I didn't get screeched in. ☹ I figured I'd be back another time when it's not a holiday and not a Ghost town on George Street, I wasn't down to get screeched in at some empty bar by a greasy kitchen staff that can't remember the requirements of the ceremony. lol But we continued to get drunk, bought a groupon on our phones to Jungle Jims, and got wasted on their drink special. Then we followed a group of people to a club called Allure. It's like a miniature Dome. Small D floor, a bar/ lookout upstairs, with a bunch of drunk college lookin kids. It filled up by the end of the night and ended a fun evening. Me and Emily made the mistake of letting her mom book the flights and it's been fun...but I'm def ready to come back! There's only so much we can do here at this time of year.

I'll send Sonja some pictures if I get any good ones. Hopefully in the new year the fellas can get together for a group photo for you. It's been a while since I've made it out with the group. There's always a few that are working or being punks and staying in a lot but that's nothing new. Can you receive parcels, like books?

RE: *Lawsuit at the end of this.*

Yah, that's fucked, they literally tested everything in that apartment, I was wondering what you would do about that, Dylan too.

A lawsuit for the time and loss of your personal belongings sounds about right to me. Good to hear you're staying on top of it and thanks for explaining the legal procedure of the case. You & Eugene put in work.

What card games have you been playing lately, learn any new ones? Have you ever played rummoli or a game called Sequence? I don't play much cards but I was introduced to those games recently and they're dope! Especially with some booze around. I'm gonna try to put some size on now as well. lol it's about fuckin time aye. Work on your handstand pushups, those are challenging.

Until next time Amigo.

Hang in there, the crew is waitin for ya.

Neither of the letters is signed, but Pookiel McCabe testified in court that he wrote them. McCabe testified he also got a phone call from Sandeson from the Burnside correctional facility after he had given his final statement to police, sometime near the beginning of 2017; he couldn't provide a date.

"First when he called me, he said like right off the bat, he said, 'I'm allowed to call you as long as we don't talk about the trial, I don't, or,'"—McCabe paused trying to remember—"something else. He said that he's allowed to call."

"What did you discuss?" asked Susan MacKay in court.

"So when we were on the phone call most of it, or all of it, was just about mutual friends that we had."

"Did you want to speak with him?"

"It was really weird having him call. I didn't really know what I would say to him, you know what I mean?"

"Okay, and about how long was the conversation?"

"Ah, around ten minutes."

On the contrary, Justin Blades testified he had no contact with Sandeson after he was arrested. He told the jury he went off the map, moved to a new address, got rid of his phone, and tried to suppress his memories of what he witnessed the night of August 15, 2015.

"The only person I really hung out with was my girlfriend. I was suppressed in a sense that I didn't see half my friends. I didn't come in contact with my family as much. Still to this date, I still have a lot to explain to them. I've just been bitter. I don't trust anyone." And then he repeated, "I don't trust anyone."

Despite his best efforts, he testified, he still hears about William Sandeson everywhere he goes. "I can't even go outside to Sobeys and not hear about it. I was there yesterday and heard about it. It's everywhere. It follows you like the plague, man."

On cross-examination, defence lawyer Eugene Tan tried to poke holes in Blades's story, but Blades held his own, at times sparring with the lawyer in front of the jury. Tan pointed Blades to a photo that showed a yellow evidence marker with a number twenty on it on the floor in the kitchen of Sandeson's apartment near some dark staining, "Do you recall if there was a pool of blood near that location?"

"Huge pool of blood. Literally it covered pretty much the whole half kitchen."

"Okay, so where would the biggest concentration have been? Right about where that staining is?" asked Tan beginning a detailed discussion of where exactly the blood was.

"I don't know what you mean—it's an abundance of blood all over the floor," said Blades, his frustration building.

"I guess what I'm asking you here is: is there like a fairly significant pool right here?"

"There's a significant pool on the whole floor!" Blades nearly shouted, exasperated.

"Is there a point to this?" asked Blades. "You just want answers?"

The judge interjected. "Mr. Blades, Mr. Tan will ask questions, and if they're questions that are not appropriate the Crown will object or I will intercede. Otherwise, you're to answer the questions."

Blades obliged but before long, he was again frustrated.

"You don't have to smoke and mirrors, it's cool," he told Tan, and was again admonished by Justice Arnold. Eugene Tan was undeterred.

"Okay, so Mr. Sandeson's running around without any particular purpose or direction at this point, is that right?"

"Yes, sir."

"Okay, is he stepping in this?"

"Definitely. There's no way not to step in it. If you're inside the apartment, you're stepping in it."

"Is it possible through that time period, that either being forced to relive this or after hearing other people talk about it that your recollection may have changed over time?"

"Well, of course, like anything you play certain things in your head. I've researched like the human psyche and if you think about things a certain way, you change things in your head, but when you see a horrific scene like that, that is burned into your head."

It was a cross-examination that seemed to help the Crown's case more than William Sandeson's.

CHAPTER 10
APPLICATION FOR MISTRIAL

On the morning of May 9, 2017, Pookiel McCabe was about to resume his testimony from the day before. He had been telling the court about what he witnessed in William Sandeson's apartment on the night of August 15, 2015. Everyone was expecting he would pick up where he had left off. Instead, defence lawyer Eugene Tan rose to address the judge with what would become the trial's most significant twist.

Tan explained that the defence had been informed the day before that an informer was inquiring about confidentiality. One of the officers working the case had advised the Crown someone was asserting that privilege. Informer privilege imposes a duty on the police, the Crown, and the courts not to release any information that risks revealing the identity of a police informer. However, Tan went on to say that it had been confirmed to his colleague, Brad Sarson, via text message the previous evening after 10 P.M. that the informer was now waiving any privilege claims. That's also when the defence learned the informer's name was Bruce Webb.

"Problem with that, my lord, is Bruce Webb is an investigator who had been employed by the investigation firm retained by defence counsel."

Bruce Webb was a retired police officer who had served thirty-five years with the RCMP and was now working as a part-time private investigator for Martin & Associates Investigations Inc., owned by Tom Martin, who was also a retired officer, having spent thirty years with Halifax Regional Police.

Lawyers often hire private investigators to act on behalf of themselves to take statements from witnesses so that they don't end up as witnesses themselves. For example, if a witness ends up on the stand saying something different than provided in the statement the lawyer could also be called to testify, but that can't happen if the lawyer wasn't the one speaking with the witness in the first place.

So it was that in the early fall of 2016, while William Sandeson's defence team was frantically preparing for his trial, Tom Martin tasked Bruce Webb with tracking down key witnesses to find out what they might say under pressure.

"Shortly thereafter, and perhaps a little suspiciously, Mr. Blades and Mr. McCabe came forward and they provided statements to the police," Tan explained. In November, when Tan received copies of the new video statements, in which Blades and McCabe now claimed to have witnessed the aftermath of murder, he confronted his private investigator.

"My instruction had been, 'When you interview them make sure that you press them a little bit so that we have a sense of what they may say under pressure.' Basically [Webb] shrugged his shoulders and he said, 'I must have leaned a little too hard.'" Tan said he asked Tom Martin to investigate further and was given the same assurances, so it seemed it was an unfortunate coincidence for the defence that the witnesses had so drastically changed their stories and the defence would just have to live with it. Tan continued his work on the case.

But now, three weeks into the trial, it appeared that William Sandeson's own investigator had turned against him and started working for the police.

On the morning of May 9, Eugene Tan told the judge that Webb had sat in on strategic defence meetings, the defence now had no idea what information he had shared with witnesses and the police, and that he believed solicitor-client privilege had been breached. Solicitor-client privilege is a right protected under the Canadian Charter of Rights and Freedoms that protects all communications between a professional legal adviser and his or her clients from being disclosed without the permission of the client. He also told the judge that Webb's employment had been terminated the night before and he was no longer taking calls from the defence.

"So in light of all that, my lord, we would be seeking a motion for a mistrial."

Justice Joshua Arnold interjected immediately. "Aren't you ahead of yourself on this?"

"Well, I would suggest, my lord, that the damage, frankly, has been done," replied Eugene Tan.

"I don't see how you're at a stage to request a mistrial when you don't know the facts yet either."

And so the court entered into another voir dire, to determine who said what and who knew what when. It would be the seventh of eleven voir dires in the Sandeson trial.

HIRED BY SANDESON'S TEAM

Bruce Webb was subpoenaed to testify in the voir dire on May 10. He told the court he had been tasked with interviewing Justin Blades and Pookiel McCabe as well as others, including Sonja Gashus, William Sandeson's girlfriend at the time. He acknowledged he had signed confidentiality agreements with Martin & Associates and that any information he would obtain would be the property of that firm.

"You understand that you had been retained by the defence?" asked Eugene Tan.

"Yes," came the response.

In fact it was Adam Sandeson, William Sandeson's brother, who put Webb in touch with Blades. Blades also testified in the voir dire that Webb told him he was trying to help Sandeson and his family. The two met on October 18, 2016.

"Do you recall how you introduced yourself?" Tan asked Webb on the stand.

"I introduced myself as a private investigator for Martin & Associates."

But what Tan really wanted to know was if Webb had encouraged Blades to go to the police.

"Mr. Blades, during the interview process and at the end, wanted to come clean. He had a real burden on his shoulders," replied Webb. "He was literally in hiding for a little over a year. It was told to him that Mr. Sandeson was getting his drugs through the Hells Angels, and he was scared to death that if he came forward he'd be killed. And when I was in his apartment, he had a knife there, he said, 'I have this knife with me all the time.' He said, 'That's why I don't have a cell plan or anything because I was scared to death.' He was really really messed up. He said, 'I'm sorry that I didn't tell the police everything at the time.'"

"All right. My question was, Mr. Webb, whether you encouraged Mr. Blades to go forward and speak to the police?"

"I said, 'Would you like to speak to the police?' and he said, 'Yes.'"

"And that's all you said? You asked him?"

"I said, 'I know a fella, and I can put you in contact.'"

"So you facilitated a meeting with the police. Is that correct?"

"Yes, I did. I felt really bad for him because he was in such a messed-up situation."

Blades corroborated that story when it was his turn on the stand.

"He wasn't just like, 'You need to go do this, but it's in your best interest.' And I think he's right," he testified.

Later the same day, Webb was driving down the road in his own neighbourhood when he saw his neighbour, a police officer, out walking with a new puppy. Webb waved him over.

Staff Sergeant Richard (Richy) Lane was in his twenty-eighth year as a police officer in Nova Scotia and was a watch commander for Halifax Regional Police at the time. He testified he wouldn't consider Webb a friend but that he would wave or say hello if he saw him in the neighbourhood. He knew that Webb worked for Tom Martin.

"How did you broach the subject with Staff Sergeant Lane? What'd you say?" Eugene Tan asked Webb in court.

"I told him that I had interviewed Justin Blades and he wanted to come forward 'cause he has more information on what occurred."

"Okay, is that all you said?"

"And I said that when he looked in the room he saw Taylor Samson's body slumped over in a chair." [Blades actually said he saw a man slumped over in a chair, a man he couldn't identify. He had never met Taylor Samson.]

"All right, so you provided some information as to what Mr. Blades might say," Tan continued.

"Yes, that was it."

"Okay, did you express to Staff Sergeant Lane that in your opinion the police weren't doing enough to further their own investigation?"

"I don't believe I did."

But Staff Sergeant Lane's testimony was contradictory.

"He knew what position I held at the time and he wanted to express a concern, I guess, that he was afraid we weren't doing enough to the investigation and he was aware of a couple witnesses that, or certainly at least one witness as I recall, that he was able to track down and provided a statement—a Mr. Blades."

"During that conversation, did he relay to you any other information such as contact information for Mr. Blades or what Mr. Blades might have to say to you?" asked Tan.

"He did at that time tell me that Mr. Blades had seen the victim dead at the table. In the same conversation, he didn't want to be involved, basically remain anonymous, so I didn't want to talk to him too much about it."

Eugene Tan wanted to know what motivated a man working for the defence to effectively switch sides.

"I was motivated by helping this young guy get his life back on track 'cause he was harbouring what he saw that night for over a year."

"Okay, so you're motivated by your desire to help Mr. Blades?"

"Yes."

"Is it also fair to say that you're motivated in part because you had come to the conclusion yourself that Mr. Sandeson was guilty?"

Long pause. "A strong likelihood yes, based on what Mr. Blades told me."

Sandeson's girlfriend, Sonja Gashus, testified that she had also met with Bruce Webb and that he had encouraged her to remove herself from the situation as much as possible, supporting her decision to decrease her communication with Sandeson. "He said that it didn't look good for Will," Gashus told the court.

"At that time, did you or did you not understand that you were subject to privilege?" Tan questioned Webb. "Were you breaking any rules of confidentiality in your own mind by doing that?"

"I believe so, I might have."

"Okay, well let's talk about that."

"With the information that he gave me in that position, I was really torn."

"You were torn, okay. So this is an emotional decision?"

"Yes."

"It wasn't a decision that you had thought about, you hadn't taken time to think about it."

"I should have taken more time to think about it. I saw Richy Lane and I talked to him right there. In hindsight, I should have contacted Tom Martin. I didn't."

Tom Martin told the court he had been in business as a private investigator since October 2011, and that his firm assisted with missing persons files, internal investigations where the clients would prefer not to have the police involved, family law especially involving the welfare of children, and a fair number of lawyer assists.

He had been retained by Walker Dunlop, one of Halifax's oldest law firms, to do a case review and locate and interview people in relation to the Sandeson file beginning in the fall of 2015. He testified Bruce Webb had been one of his senior investigators for nearly four years and would have signed a confidentiality agreement drawn up by his firm's lawyers, an agreement he believed Webb had breached in a serious manner.

"It's just a promise on the investigator's part to hold and keep confidential the nature of any business that they may learn through the course of their employment with myself."

Martin also testified he was aware Blades and McCabe had gone to the police shortly after Webb interviewed them.

"It caused me to have a conversation with Mr. Webb in which I asked him, did he in any way, shape, or form suggest or direct Mr. Blades to contact the police?"

"And did you get a response from Mr. Webb?" Tan asked.

"I did."

"And his response was?"

"Absolutely not."

Martin went on to say that Webb provided no explanation as to why his interview and the statements appeared to have come fairly close in time.

"I can only speak for myself and I just assumed that they went to the police."

"What was your reaction to Mr. Webb's denial?"

"I believed him," said Martin.

"Okay, based on what?" questioned Tan.

"Based on the fact that I knew the man, and he'd worked for me for a few years."

It was because of that belief, he said, that he didn't share this information with defence counsel. He did speak with Webb about the matter again but not until two nights before the testimony.

"I told him that I wasn't happy learning that he was a confidential source for the police."

"And did he respond?"

"Yes."

"What did he say?"

"He told me that that was not the case, and I said, 'Tell me what's the case,' and he explained to me that he had interviewed Mr. Blades. Mr. Blades was the only individual discussed. He had interviewed Mr. Blades and Mr. Blades had said he'd wanted to contact the police and he wanted Mr. Webb to make that happen for him. I asked Mr. Webb, 'Why didn't you tell me about this?' And he said he made a mistake."

Webb admitted that throughout the course of the investigation he would have been privy to strategic meetings and information that would have been considered to be privileged.

"Did he tell you how he came about this information?" Tan asked Sergeant Lane.

"He told me he had interviewed [Blades]."

"Did he say in what capacity? Like, whether he had done so as an investigator?"

"He didn't, but I assumed so."

"Did you have any thoughts or inklings as to who his client might have been?"

"I would assume the accused."

"Okay, did that raise any concerns with you, the fact that somebody retained by the accused was offering information to the police?"

"Do you want my opinion on it?" Lane asked.

"Yes, I'm asking for your thoughts at that time."

"I got the feeling he knew the accused was guilty and didn't want him to get away with it. That's the perception I got from him."

"Okay, now in terms of your own thoughts and considerations about it, the fact that this information came about as a result of his retainer by the accused, did that weigh on your mind at all?"

"I'm more of a as-long-as-the-truth-gets-out kinda guy so that's basically why I said, 'I'll get somebody to get in touch with ya.' He believed he was telling me factual information and it was part of this case and it was the truth and it needed to get out in court, so that's why I set him up with the investigators."

Lane spoke with Corporal Allison and another officer working the case, and Allison, who admitted police otherwise had no plans to speak with Blades again, called Bruce Webb the following day.

"He didn't give me many details, just that Justin had disclosed to him something that was very troubling to him," Allison told the court. "He said Justin was messed up from what he witnessed. He also said that Justin witnessed something that happened in the apartment."

They all agreed to meet at Blades's house. "I went there to introduce him to then Constable Allison, it was about noon on the twentieth, and they left in the car and that was it," Webb told the court.

The same day Webb would track down another witness, Pookiel McCabe. Three days after that, the two would speak over the phone, as McCabe had moved to Ontario.

Webb told McCabe he had been talking with Blades and relayed some of the information Blades had given him. He did not tell McCabe that Blades was going to be in touch with police. Again, Webb encouraged the witness to go to the police but this time, received no commitment. The investigator passed on contact particulars to Corporal Allison.

"What motivated you to do it on that occasion?" Tan asked while Webb was on the stand.

"I wanted to do the right thing."

"You wanted to do the right thing. And by doing the right thing you had concluded that Mr. Sandeson was guilty?"

"A strong possibility."

"A strong possibility. Right, so that was your conclusion."

"There were two witnesses," Webb offered.

"Right, but my question being that you had reached your conclusion, is that correct?"

After a long pause, Webb quietly responded, "Yes."

Detective Constable Roger Sayer, Sergeant Derrick Boyd, and Corporal Jody Allison all testified that they travelled to Toronto to interview Pookiel McCabe and showed up at his home with the assistance of some Ontario officers.

"It was really really early in the morning," McCabe testified.

"We surprised Mr. McCabe. There was no arrangements made with him at all," Allison testified.

Tan asked McCabe if he believed he had any choice but to go with police to provide another statement when they showed up at his door. He said that he believed he did.

"Why did you choose to participate?"

"Because it was the right thing to do."

Blades and McCabe went on to give police the best evidence they would obtain, bolstering their case against William Sandeson.

"I'm going to suggest to you, sir, that you sort of knew that what you were doing was wrong," Eugene Tan accused Bruce Webb.

He paused.

"Yes," he finally answered.

"Right. You did. And that's borne out in the fact that you were asking for confidentiality from the police."

"Yes."

Corporal Allison had previously told the court that Webb had been requesting confidentiality from the beginning and that he had asked that his name not be used in any fashion. Detective Constable Sayer also said he was aware Webb had requested anonymity. "If somebody makes that request I will honour it," he said.

Somehow something still got confused.

"You asked for privilege, which you've since waived," Tan continued probing Webb.

There was no response.

"Since that time you have elected not to pursue that?" Tan pressed.

Again, there was no response. Tan waited.

"I don't recall that," Webb said finally, and everyone in the courtroom knew there was a problem.

"Sorry, my lord, I was advised that it was no longer being asserted," Tan offered the judge.

"We're going to stand down now. Mr. Webb, you'll remain under oath, and I'm just going to have you wait outside the courtroom while I chat with the lawyers."

"Well, my lord," Tan began.

The judge interrupted, firmly.

"We're going to take a break right now, Mr. Tan, and you and the Crown are going to have a chat and you're going to sort this out, you're going to find out where this information came from and where the assertion that confidentiality and privilege was waived, because clearly Mr. Webb is indicating that it was not. And then we're going to resume and you're going to explain to me what's going on here."

Susan MacKay jumped in. "I can do that without a break, my lord, right now."

"Okay, Ms. MacKay."

"My lord, I spoke with Corporal Allison, I think it's two nights ago now, around suppertime. He indicated to me on the phone that Mr. Webb had agreed to waive privilege, the claim of privilege, confidentiality. That's what I was told."

"This is not a knee-jerk-reaction situation. We have somebody on the stand who has just said under oath that they were not waiving their confidentiality, their privilege," said the judge.

He stood court down and ultimately decided to enter into a voir dire within a voir dire, essentially a trial within a trial within a trial, to determine whether Bruce Webb could claim informer privilege.

"It's a sensitive issue and, although it may be trying to put the cat back into the bag, that is not possible," said Justice Arnold. Although Webb's name had already been published, Arnold held the voir dire in camera, excluding the press and all members of the public from the courtroom. (At this time as all live reporting had ceased, social media was rife with rumours as to what was taking place. Many thought Sandeson must be changing his plea.) Lawyers were directed not to discuss his decision, and it was not released publicly until August 25, 2017, well after the trial had concluded.

Justice Josh Arnold ruled Bruce Webb could have no expectation of privacy under the circumstances.

"While the identity of confidential informers must be closely guarded, if Webb ever was a source or confidential informant in these circumstances, once he met with the police and Blades together to introduce them and to assist in making Blades comfortable such that he would provide a statement to the police, he lost any possible status as a confidential informant," Arnold wrote.

"Webb was not merely a citizen who quietly provided the police with information about criminal activity with the expectation of confidentiality. Instead he became an active participant in the criminal investigation and as such is not a source or a confidential informant."

In May 2017, with no explanation as to why or how, the original voir dire continued and the public was welcomed back inside the courtroom.

Bruce Webb took the stand again, but this time he was not questioned by Eugene Tan, because in yet another bizarre twist, the lead lawyer announced he would also become a witness in the voir dire, meaning he could not be present while Webb was being examined by his colleague, Brad Sarson. Sarson could also not be the one to question Tan, so yet another Halifax lawyer joined the growing chorus of defence lawyers who now had their hands in the Sandeson trial.

Sarson began by reminding Webb he had previously testified he had stopped to speak with Staff Sergeant Richard Lane while he was out walking a puppy.

"What you didn't mention earlier, in your earlier testimony, was an earlier conversation that took place at Staff Sergeant Lane's house in relation to this matter. Do you recall that?"

"Yes."

"And my understanding is that that would have taken place sometime prior to you approaching Staff Sergeant Lane on October 20, 2016," Sarson said.

"That would be in the fall of 2015," Webb agreed.

"So perhaps a year or so previous?"

"Yes."

"And had you already become involved in relation to the Sandeson matter at that time?"

"Yes."

"And my understanding is that you went to Staff Sergeant Lane's house?"

"Yes."

"What was your purpose in going to his residence?"

"I wanted to get a better feel for the investigation."

"What do you mean by that?"

"I was hoping I could get a read from Staff Sergeant Lane on the investigation."

"To what end?" Sarson continued.

"To what end? To get a feel on what the regional police had because at that time the information that we had was very sketchy."

"Okay, would it surprise you if I said to you that Staff Sergeant Lane testified that you had gone there to inquire whether the police were doing everything they could in order to prosecute the case or gather evidence to prosecute the case?"

"No, that wouldn't surprise me."

"Okay, so do you agree that that in fact happened?"

"Yes."

"Okay, so a minute ago you just said you went there to sort of get some idea—"

Webb interrupted. "Exactly, and in the conversation was, 'cause we were bantering back and forth, you know, 'Are you doing everything?'"

"Okay, by asking that question what were you hoping the answer was going to be?

"I don't know."

"Well, were you hopeful that the police were doing a shoddy job and therefore they would have a more difficult time proving their case, or were you fearful that they were doing a shoddy job and were looking to assist them in gathering evidence?"

"No, I was just there to glean some information," Webb said.

"Okay, did you express any opinion to Staff Sergeant Lane at that time with respect to your opinion as it regards to Mr. Sandeson's guilt or innocence?"

"Yes."

"Okay. And what did you indicate to Staff Sergeant Lane at that time?"

"It appeared that Mr. Sandeson's case wasn't really good for him."

"Meaning you felt he was guilty?"

"Did I feel he was guilty? Just based on the facts we had it didn't look good for Mr. Sandeson."

All of this was happening unbeknownst to the jury, who had been sent home.

Seated beside his legal team, William Sandeson took notes, as Webb explained the role he had played in his case.

"You'd agree with me that there's a difference between someone being guilty and the Crown being able to prove that they're guilty?" Sarson continued.

"Yes."

"All right, and were your comments more directed toward the Crown being able to prove a case against Mr. Sandeson or Mr. Sandeson's actual guilt?"

"I don't know."

"You don't know because you don't recall what your thought was at that time?"

"Precisely."

"You may recall, you testified earlier, that part of your motivation at least in approaching the police was a belief that you would rather see a guilty person go to jail than have a murderer walk free. Correct?"

"No. After I interviewed Justin Blades, he was very distraught and he wanted to come clean with the information he had. I also felt at that point that if I didn't come forward then I would be obstructing justice."

"I'm going to suggest to you sir that on earlier occasions you had testified that part of your motivations going to the police was because you did not want to see a guilty man walk free."

"I did not say that," Webb maintained earnestly.

Sarson moved on.

"As part of your assignment being involved in this investigation you would have sat in on a number of meetings, is that correct?"

"That's correct."

"Do you remember how many meetings that you would have attended where Mr. Sandeson's case was the topic of discussion?"

"Several."

"And during those meetings there would have been a number of topics discussed. Correct?"

"Correct."

"And that would have included a review of Crown disclosure?"

"Yes?"

"It would have included discussion of defence strategy?"

"I really wasn't sure what the defence strategy was," Webb replied.

"Okay, so there had been no discussion with respect to Mr. Blades and Mr. McCabe as being 'wildcards' or being 'unknowns'?"

"Yeah, they were unknowns, yes."

"Do you recall being present for any meetings where there were legal arguments discussed with respect to attacking the search or any of the statements being given by Mr. Sandeson?"

"Yes."

"Were you aware of the defence's intention to attack the search of Mr. Sandeson's apartment?"

"Yes."

"Were you aware of the defence's intention to attack the admissibility of the statements Mr. Sandeson had given to the police?"

"I believe so, yes."

On cross-examination Webb testified he did not share any of that information with the police.

Sarson asked Webb if he reviewed Blades's first statement to police before he interviewed him. He did not, but he was aware of the gist of its contents.

"In particular that they had claimed not to have seen anything?" Sarson asked.

"Yes."

"Had you formulated any opinion as to whether those statements were accurate or honest?"

"I didn't think they were honest statements."

"And what did you base that on?"

"The look on their face when they looked in the apartment on the video."

Webb was referencing the surveillance video captured in the hallway outside Sandeson's apartment building in which Justin Blades can be seen looking inside the apartment in the minutes following the murder. He appears to be shocked.

On November 8, following Webb's interviews with Blades and McCabe and following their final statements to the police, Webb met with his boss, Tom Martin, and Sandeson's legal team to present the results of his interview. The defence was not yet aware the witnesses had gone to the police with statements that would sink their case. In that meeting, Webb didn't tell the lawyers and Martin he had gone to police or that he encouraged Blades and McCabe to go to the police.

"Was there any discussion during that meeting of some additional information coming from the Crown with respect to Mr. Blades or Mr. McCabe?" asked Sarson.

"I don't recall that."

"Do you recall a telephone call with Mr. Tan a couple of days later on November 10, 2016?"

"I don't recall that."

"So if I were to suggest to you that you had a telephone call with Mr. Tan wherein he outlined to you that he had received new statements from the police, one from Mr. Blades, one from Mr. McCabe, and he questioned you about what you had said to them, does that assist you in recalling whether you had a telephone call with Mr. Tan?"

Webb cut him of. "I don't remember any phone call with Mr. Tan. I'm sorry."

"Do you recall Mr. Tan at any point in time asking you whether or not you had told Mr. McCabe or Mr. Blades to contact the police or go to the police?"

"I don't recall that, I don't recall speaking with Mr. Tan on the phone. After that meeting, I don't recall speaking with him."

"What about a conversation with Mr. Martin after November 8, 2016? Do you recall having a conversation with Mr. Martin or Mr. Martin confronting you with what you might have done or said to have led Mr. Blades and Mr. McCabe to the police?"

"No, I do not."

"So you're saying that you never were put in a position where you had to lie to either Mr. Martin or Mr. Tan with respect to your actions as far as going to the police or encouraging Mr. Blades or Mr. McCabe to go to the police," Sarson said.

"I didn't volunteer the information and I wasn't asked."

"So if I were to suggest to you that you were confronted and you had lied and said that in fact you weren't sure why they had gone to the police, there must have been a coincidence or you leaned too hard on them or something to that effect, you would disagree with that or you don't remember that?"

"I don't remember that."

On cross-examination, Crown attorney Susan MacKay asked Bruce Webb only a couple of questions—whether he had communicated to Blades and McCabe any of the information he had gleaned from defence meetings and whether he had communicated the same information to the police. In both cases, he said he had not.

Bruce Webb was free to go but before the defence called its own lawyer, Justice Arnold wanted an explanation for this highly unusual move with regard to the relevance of the evidence Eugene Tan would provide. Sarson explained that since the Crown was proposing to argue the defence had an obligation to pursue disclosure, meaning they should have asked about Bruce Webb's involvement when they became suspicious, the defence should have an opportunity to show they did their due diligence. That seemed to satisfy the judge, and Sandeson's lead lawyer was sworn in as a witness to be questioned by Mark Knox, another Halifax defence lawyer who had had no involvement with the case to this point. The testimony was brief.

"We've heard about two recent contentious statements of Mr. McCabe and Mr. Blades," Mark Knox began. "You're aware of those two statements?"

"I am aware of those," replied Tan.

"And on November 8th of 2016 [when Tan met with Webb for an update in the case] were those two statements in your hands?"

"They came to me later that day, after the time that I had met with Mr. Webb."

"And what, if anything did you do with respect to contacting Mr. Webb after you got the statements?"

"Well my recollection is that I met with Mr. Webb and others early in the afternoon, about 1 P.M. I received the copies of the statements on CD, so video statements, no transcripts, late that afternoon. I did have an opportunity to review them the following day. That would have been November 9th. On November 10th, I had that opportunity to review them and I was somewhat surprised that these statements had been taken. As a result of my surprise, I phoned Mr. Webb, I believe the number that I had for him was a cellphone. He and I exchanged a call or two and then I was able to finally speak to him I believe sometime mid- to late afternoon on the 10th."

"Okay so you actually spoke to him on this occasion, true?"

"I did, yes," confirmed Tan.

It was the complete opposite testimony provided by Bruce Webb just moments earlier.

"Okay, and what was the essence of the conversation?" Knox continued.

"The essence of the conversation was that I had been surprised that police statements had been taken, particularly in such relative close proximity to the time that he had met with two of those witnesses, Mr. McCabe and Mr. Blades. I understand that he conducted his work between the 20th and 30th of October. These statements came at roughly that time frame, or shortly thereafter. I was surprised. I said to him, 'Bruce, what happened here? What's going on? Why would they have gone to the police?' His response to me was, 'You had told me to lean on them and I guess I leaned too hard.' I should say that my instructions to him were in fact that he should be somewhat aggressive with them to see what they may or may not say if placed under pressure."

"Okay, thank you, Mr. Tan. Those are the questions that I have."

The cross-examination went a little longer, a rare opportunity for a prosecutor to question her legal opponent.

"Mr. Tan, did you listen to the statement of Justin Blades in its entirety before you spoke with Mr. Webb?" asked Susan MacKay.

"Yes, I did."

"Okay, and so in there you saw that toward the end of the statement, he said, 'I think you guys have that number maybe. I gave it to Bruce.' And then the answer to that being, 'Yeah.' And then he said some other things and that he made reference three times to 'Bruce' in there."

"Correct."

"And in fact how good it had felt to speak with Bruce," MacKay persisted.

"Right," agreed Tan.

"Did it not make you think that there was a link there between Bruce Webb and the police having his phone number and contacting Mr. Blades?"

"No, not at all."

"Why not?" MacKay asked.

"The heart of the matter that Mr. Webb was retained for was one of confidentiality. He was under specific instructions, he had an agreement with the investigator that I had hired, I had met Mr. Webb in the past, I understood what his background was, I had been assured that confidentiality would be a top issue. Mr. Martin, who is the lead investigator that I had hired, had assured me in the past that confidentiality would be maintained. Mr. Martin had reviewed with me his specific instructions to his investigators. I was satisfied that there would not be any breaches of those protocols, so when I saw Mr. Webb's name or when I heard Mr. Webb's name, when I heard 'Bruce' I certainly said, 'That is a little bit of a concern,' but frankly it was also consistent with him having leaned on them, and Mr. Blades having made a decision to go forward. So I didn't question that he would have broken his confidentiality."

"And you did not ask the Crown about whether there was any connection either, did you?"

"No, I had no reason to. I understood the Crown had an obligation to disclose that."

"What did you make of the statement that the police would have Justin's number because he had given it to Bruce? What did you make of that statement?"

"I didn't consider that at all at the time quite frankly. Mr. Blades was one that I had been advised in the past was somewhat easily confused and so I didn't make anything of it."

"Thank you. Those are the questions for the Crown."

That concluded the evidence the judge would hear in the application for a mistrial. The lawyers got set to argue their case. The defence was up first.

Over the course of several hours, with the judge interjecting to ask questions every step of the way, Brad Sarson argued the mistrial application was based on three grounds, late disclosure by the Crown, an alleged breach of solicitor-client privilege by Bruce Webb, and William Sandeson's right to a fair trial.

"The defence takes the position that it should be uncontested that the Crown had an obligation to disclose this," Sarson declared, referring to the fact the Crown didn't inform the defence of the existence of a tipster, and further about what it knew about Bruce Webb's role in facilitating the statements Blades and McCabe gave to the police, and therefore breaching William Sandeson's constitutional right.

The police have an obligation to disclose the evidence they collect to the Crown and the Crown has an obligation to disclose that information to the defence, but in this case the Crown argued it didn't disclose the information because it believed the defence already knew.

"The Crown's position is that the statement itself discloses Mr. Webb's involvement," MacKay argued, referencing the several times Justin Blades referred to "Bruce" in the statement which was provided to the defence in November 2016.

"The defence either should have known that Bruce Webb was involved, or if they actually did not realize this, they should have at the very least been alerted by the statement's content, that Mr. Webb may very well have been. So they should have followed up on this in an appropriate manner."

Sarson said that it was easy to see the connection in hindsight. "Hindsight's 20/20 as they say."

Justice Arnold pointed out that while the name "Bruce" is mentioned in the statement, the extent of his involvement and the actions he took is not, but the Crown said it couldn't share that because it learned when everyone else did, when the witnesses were on the stand.

Sarson reminded the judge that the defence did confront both Bruce Webb and his employer, Tom Martin, to inquire about the strange coincidence.

"So defence maintains that defence took appropriate steps to ascertain whether something untoward had occurred."

But, Susan MacKay pointed out that the defence did not contact the Crown to ask what may have happened or Justin Blades himself. On that point, the judge also had some questions for the defence.

"Why wouldn't the defence write to the Crown and say, 'Is there something that I should know about here?'" he asked Sarson.

Sarson maintained it never occurred to the defence to do so because it never occurred to the lawyers that Webb would act in this fashion.

"I can say, having done research on this issue, I can say that I haven't encountered a case where a private investigator retained by the defence decided to actively work for the police, which is essentially what Mr. Webb did, and assist in the creation of evidence and lead that evidence to the police. Couldn't find a single case where that had happened. So for the court to suggest that it should have been somewhat obvious that Mr. Webb had acted in this capacity—"

"I'm not suggesting that it should have been obvious," said Arnold. "I'm suggesting that the comments here make it clear that either Mr. Blades was mixed up about who Mr. Webb was working with or for or what Mr. Webb's involvement was or that he clearly felt that Mr. Webb and the police were communicating for some reason."

"Yes, and I would suggest that the defence showed diligence by confronting Mr. Webb and Mr. Martin confronting Mr. Webb," said Sarson.

"Well did anybody call Mr. Blades, who was clearly co-operating with everybody who had spoke to him at that point, to ask him why he was mentioning 'Bruce' throughout this statement?"

"No."

"Why not?" Arnold asked. "He wanted to speak to everybody. He spoke to Mr. Webb, he spoke to the police, he wanted to apologize to Mr. Samson's mother. I mean, why didn't the defence just pick up the phone and call him, and say, 'Why are you mentioning Bruce all over this statement?'"

Sarson responded that the defence simply assumed that after Blades told the story once [to Webb], he decided to go to the police of his own volition. Sarson told the judge if the defence had been aware of the information in a timely fashion it would have requested that the statements of Blades and McCabe be ruled inadmissible before the trial began.

"The difficulty here, of course, is that before the issue was fully realized or the impact of the issue was fully realized Mr. McCabe had already testified in front of the jury."

Sarson went on to say that giving the defence another chance to question some of the witnesses who had already testified was also not an appropriate remedy for the problem because it would give the jury the impression that the defence was desperate or that something had gone wrong.

"The clumsy sequence of events in this case cannot help but result in confusion in the community as well as skepticism about the efficacy of the jury system," he explained. "The importance of the public's confidence in the Canadian jury system and in the administration of justice simply cannot be overstated. This public trust, respect, and acceptance if eroded will be at great cost to the effective operation of the criminal justice system."

The defence also argued that Bruce Webb was subject to solicitor-client privilege, and that he not only alerted the police but essentially created the evidence now before the jury in the form of testimony from Blades and McCabe.

The judge asked the defence whether Webb would have been obstructing justice, as he feared, if he had not told the police what Blades and McCabe had shared with him. "What were his legal obligations?" he asked.

"He had no legal obligations I would suggest," Sarson responded.

"Based on what?"

"The analogy I would draw is, lawyer represents a client on a domestic assault, lawyer interviews complainant to find out before court what she may say in court, complainant tells lawyer, 'yeah, not only did it happen but your client has contacted me on three occasions telling me I shouldn't go to court.' Lawyer has now become aware of arguably a new offence by his or her client and I would suggest the lawyer has no obligation to contact the Crown or police or make the Crown or police aware of that information, that that information is still subject to solicitor-client privilege.

"I'm saying that whether the information is given to the private investigator or given to the lawyer directly, there is no difference. And, just as a lawyer who receives information of a further offence having been committed by his or her client is under no obligation to go to the police or the Crown, neither is the private investigator," Sarson continued.

The Crown argued Webb was not subject to solicitor-client privilege at all as that privilege protects only communication between a client and his solicitor, or lawyer, but the defence argued further that the police would never have located Blades and McCabe if not for the actions of Bruce Webb.

"What we're dealing with here are the Halifax Regional Police and the RCMP," said Justice Arnold. "We have Mr. Blades who has testified that he was working."

"Mmhmm," said Sarson.

"At the hospital."

"Yep."

"In the emergency department."

"Yes."

"And that he was fighting sporadically professionally in public."

(Justin Blades testified that he was an avid mixed martial arts competitor before he got involved with track and field and even competed internationally.)

"Yes."

"Are you really suggesting to me that this would have been a stretch for the police to have located Mr. Blades? Is that really the position that you're putting to me?"

"There had been no contact with him since—" Sarson began.

"I understand that he hadn't raised the flag and said, 'here I am,'" Arnold interjected.

"Right."

"Or that he hadn't given them forwarding information, so is it your position that the police are only able to locate individuals who have given them forwarding information?"

"No."

"I just have a tough time with this, Mr. Sarson, that the police wouldn't have been able to locate these guys, at least Mr. Blades. He was working, in a hospital, and he was fighting professionally."

"Ability to locate and motivation to locate are two different things, I would suggest," said Sarson.

"Sure, yes."

"So, I don't want to contest their ability to locate him, but I would contest their motivation to locate him."

"Okay."

Naturally, the Crown countered that while the police had no plans to re-interview Blades and McCabe, they never believed they hadn't seen anything, and both men were always on the Crown's witness list and would have been subpoenaed to testify eventually.

"The Crown submits that the information he provided was discoverable to the Crown in that it very likely would have eventually come to light to the police, but probably just closer to the actual start of the trial," MacKay said.

Finally the defence argued there was simply no way forward because William Sandeson's right to a fair trial had been jeopardized, first pointing out the police were aware Webb was working for the defence but still made efforts to seek out information from him.

"What are they supposed to do?" questioned Arnold. "Are they supposed to say, 'Hey I can't talk to you?' Are they supposed to say, 'I'm not going to go follow up with this witness who's provided us a statement that said something very different?' What are their obligations?"

"At the very least, I would suggest the police had an obligation to take more steps than what they did."

"Which would be—"

"Consulting the Crown for instance."

For its part, the Crown argued while the defence may have no legal duty to get to the truth of the matter, the police do have a duty to investigate and reinvestigate until they find out what actually happened. Susan MacKay went on to acknowledge that while it was certainly unfortunate for the defence that the private investigator decided to tip off the police, it wasn't unfair.

"Bottom line is, the right to a fair trial does not equate to a right to the most favourable trial possible," MacKay proclaimed, but the defence persisted in its request for a new trial.

"And then what?" asked the judge.

"If there's a mistrial?" Sarson responded.

"Yeah."

"As in any mistrial, the Crown has the right to elect to retry."

"But what about the evidence, the evidence that you're complaining about?" Arnold continued.

"A trial judge would hold a voir dire to determine whether it's admissible or not, I would suggest."

"And a request that neither Mr. Blades nor Mr. McCabe be allowed to testify? Is that what the remedy would be?"

"Well, that would be the remedy sought," Sarson agreed.

"Okay, can you show me a case somewhere where witnesses

were not allowed to testify based on a Section 7 or 11 violation?" Arnold referred to the sections of the Canadian Charter of Rights and Freedoms that protect a person's legal rights.

"No," he paused, "not that I've encountered." He paused again, before forging ahead with more.

"But this is part of the problem. Because of the way disclosure has unfolded, defence, mid-trial, is scrambling to address a number of issues. The entire order of the trial has been thrown out of whack...I think all parties would agree that this trial has been anything but smooth in the way it's unfolded."

On that, everyone did seem to agree.

Still, after taking some time to consider all of the evidence presented by both sides, five days later, Justice Joshua Arnold denied Sandeson's request for a new trial. "I do not think that it's necessary. I don't think that there will be a miscarriage of justice if a mistrial is not declared."

Later in a written decision, Arnold stated the Crown was obliged to disclose the specific fact of Webb's contact with the police, and failed to do so in a timely fashion, but that the defence also did not diligently pursue disclosure of the identity or involvement of "Bruce" in the statements. Arnold felt any infringement of Sandeson's right to a fair trial as a result of the late disclosure in this case was at the lower end of the scale. Further, Arnold ruled Webb's communications with the police did not amount to a breach of solicitor-client privilege or litigation privilege.

Justice Arnold did offer a remedy for the late disclosure "in these very unusual circumstances." He offered to adjourn the trial in order to allow Sandeson time to consider whom he may wish to re-cross-examine in the case and then an opportunity to conduct that additional cross-examination of witnesses prior to the Crown closing its case.

Sandeson refused the offer.

And so, the trial continued.

CHAPTER 11

THE CROWN'S CASE: FRIEND OR FOE

"The next witness is Chantale Comeau," said Susan MacKay.

A number of people who knew William Sandeson, perhaps even considered him a friend, were dragged into the trial to tell the jury what they knew about his whereabouts in the days following the murder.

Chantale Comeau was a twenty-three-year-old Dalhousie student, poised to graduate the following week with a bachelor of arts. In the summer of 2015, she was working at Starbucks in downtown Halifax with William Sandeson's girlfriend, Sonja Gashus. Gashus regularly drove her to work. She didn't know Sandeson very well but said she had met him. On the morning of Sunday, August 16, she thought it was odd that Sandeson was driving and Gashus was in the passenger's seat.

Comeau testified Sandeson was wearing a hunter-orange hat and what she thought was a big jacket or hoodie with sweatpants.

"Hey, Will, why do you have a hat on? It's like fifteen degrees or so outside," Comeau said she said to Sandeson when he picked her up. She said Sandeson just kind of shrugged off her comment. On cross-examination by the defence, Comeau retracted that statement, saying she didn't believe she made a comment about the weather after all.

She said the only conversation on the short drive to the Starbucks on Queen Street was about what Sandeson and Gashus had had to eat at the Stubborn Goat the night before and what Comeau had had when she went there previously.

Comeau said the car was the same car Gashus always drove, but that there were a bunch of things in the back seat. She couldn't recall what was in the back seat but testified they were things that weren't usually there.

Comeau's testimony was brief.

SANDESON'S ROOMMATE TAKES STAND

Dylan Zinck-Selig, twenty-four, testified he was William Sandeson's roommate in August 2015. They had been living together since September 2014, but Zinck-Selig testified he wasn't spending much time at the Henry Street apartment because he was with his girlfriend. He went back a couple of times a week to let his cat out. Will also had a cat and Zinck-Selig testified he let both cats out through his bedroom window. That's the same window through which Sandeson told police Morphsuited intruders entered the apartment and killed Taylor Samson.

"I'm going to take you back to Friday, August 14th," Kim McOnie told Zinck-Selig. "Can you tell us what, if any, contact you had with Will Sandeson on that day?"

"I believe he told me not to come home past eight o'clock the following day," said Zinck-Selig, telling the court he was confident in the information, just not entirely clear through which method he received that message.

"And was it usual or unusual to get that sort of request from Mr. Sandeson?"

"For a whole night it was unusual. Usually it would be an hour, twenty minutes, tops."

Zinck-Selig did not question Sandeson about the odd request.

He was last at the apartment he shared with Sandeson around 7:30 P.M. on Saturday, August 15. No one else was home at that time and he didn't notice anything about the window in his bedroom.

Zinck-Selig said the next time he was at his apartment was at 11:30 P.M. on Sunday, August 16. Zinck-Selig said when he first arrived back at the Henry Street apartment, no one was there. Sandeson arrived about twenty minutes later, his girlfriend shortly after.

"Do you recall what you talked about?"

"Just about how the apartment was clean, and he mentioned he threw out the shower curtain," Zinck-Selig testified, somewhat hesitantly.

He said Sandeson and Gashus went to bed. He left around 1:30 A.M., picked up his girlfriend, and went back to her apartment. He didn't return to Henry Street until Tuesday or Wednesday and he wasn't allowed in. He didn't know why at the time.

He told the court he believed he messaged Will Sandeson on Monday to ask if he was home. There was no response and he has had no contact with him since then.

On cross-examination, Brad Sarson asked Dylan Zinck-Selig about the window in his bedroom. Zinck-Selig confirmed he and Sandeson would use the window to access a barbeque on the roof. He also confirmed that while there was no stair access to the roof, there were stairs on the adjacent building and it was a fairly easy climb over the handrail to get to the roof outside his bedroom window. He said he had done it himself. Sarson was trying to show the jury that the story Sandeson told police about intruders entering that way was possible.

Sarson also asked Zinck-Selig if it surprised him when Sandeson told him he threw out the shower curtain.

"No, it didn't," Zinck-Selig replied.

TOP: Will Sandeson in provincial court in Halifax in October 2015. The aspiring doctor apppeared briefly as the court set dates for a preliminary hearing.

BOTTOM: Sandeson family members at his bail hearing. Left to right: father, Michael; mother, Laurie; and brother Adam.

Defence lawyer Eugene Tan, who knew the Sandeson family through sports.

Statement from the Sandeson Family

We are disappointed and disturbed by
the Crown's use of subpoenas to keep
us out of the courtroom for the entire
trial period.

In March, we were issued 2 subpoenas
commanding us to appear as witnesses for
the Prosecution between April 18 and June 13
Under the exclusion of witness process,
anyone subpoenad is not allowed to be
present in the courtroom until after giving
testimony. We were never called as witnesses.
Therefore, we were kept away for the entire
duration.

A note that the Sandeson family passed to reporters during the trial,
expressing their displeasure with the court proceedings.

TOP: Taylor's mother, Linda Boutilier, and her son, Connor. Boutilier was a strong advocate for Taylor throughout the justice process, once shouting at Sandeson and demanding to know where her son's body was.

BOTTOM LEFT: Taylor Samson grade two school photo.

BOTTOM RIGHT: Taylor in a Halloween costume.

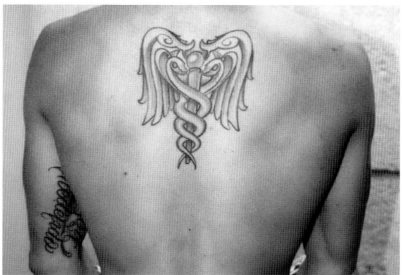

TOP: Taylor Samson's stepmother, Karen Burke; his father, Dean Samson; Crown attorneys Susan MacKay and Kim McOnie talk outside the courtroom as jurors deliberate at Nova Scotia Supreme Court on June 17, 2017. *BOTTOM:* Will Sandeson's back tattoo, which resembles a symbol for medicine. Before he was accepted at Dalhousie, Sandeson briefly attended a med school in the Caribbean.

Taylor Samson's friends and family are relieved and emotional after the first-degree murder verdict.

TOP: An exhibit photo showing an area near Truro searched by police. Court heard that Taylor Samson's DNA was found on a number of items seized from the Sandeson family farm, including a shower curtain, a duffle bag, and garbage bags.

BOTTOM: Will Sandeson's car, a black Mazda Protegé. He was seen on video loading garbage bags and a blue Adidas bag into the trunk the day his phone had pinged in the Truro area.

The author and Taylor Samson's mother, Linda Boutilier, after the trial.

"And that was because there was some mould on the shower curtain?"

"Yes, there was."

Dylan Zinck-Selig was free to go.

THE WEED

"Next witness is Nick Rotta-Loria," said Kim McOnie.

Rotta-Loria was twenty-five years old and in the midst of finishing his PhD in chemistry at Dal. He told the jury he lived upstairs in the same building as Adam Sandeson, William Sandeson's brother. On the morning of Monday, August 17, Rotta-Loria said he was at work at a lab at Dal when he got a call from Adam to move his car because Will had his motorcycle parked at the back of the house.

"I just walked over to the house, moved my car, had a quick chat with Will about his schedule for med school, just kind of chit-chatting about this and that, and then I went back to work."

Two days later, Rotta-Loria testified he ran into a girl he had tutored who was really upset.

"I asked her what happened. She told me that she'd found out that Taylor had been killed." He drove her home and then went home himself. Adam Sandeson and his girlfriend were there.

"I told them. I said I'd run into a girl, she told me Taylor had been killed, and Adam said, 'Yeah, I just got off the phone with my dad a few minutes ago and Will's up on first-degree murder charges.'"

That's when Adam's other roommate, Matt Donovan, came into the living room. It was around midnight on Wednesday.

"We were chatting about it and then Matt kind of said, 'Should we tell him what's in the basement?' to which I said, 'What is in the basement?'"

The group headed downstairs and discovered three items: a Dal Track and Field backpack, a KitchenAid box, and a plastic bag.

"I put on a pair of gloves and I opened the backpack and in it were what looked like freezer bags of weed."

Rotta-Loria said, not knowing what to do, he and his friends went back upstairs and agreed they would sleep on it. The next day Rotta-Loria and Donovan decided they needed to take action. "We knew this had something to do, we figured this had something to do, with the case," Rotta-Loria told the jury.

He decided to call a lawyer who advised the group how to give statements to the police. When they went home they found the drug squad going through the house.

Detective Constable Illya Nielsen, with HRP's Forensic Identification Unit, told the jury he executed the drug search warrant. He did a walkthrough of the entire residence, photographing each room as it was before police began their search. He went through those photos for the jury, identifying each room. One of the photos was of a Morphsuit, which was considered an item of interest and found hanging in a closet in the apartment. No one ever explained why it was there.

Nielsen testified he found a taped-up box, a backpack, and a green grocery bag inside a closet in the basement.

"I used a scalpel to cut the tape open on the top of the box," Nielsen testified. Inside he found two vacuum-sealed bags with markings and black marker on the top with what appeared to be marijuana inside. He said there were similar bags in the backpack. He found fingerprints on the box and the bags, but they didn't match Sandeson's or Samson's. The fingerprints were also run nationally against anyone who has a criminal record in Canada. There were no matches.

Nielsen also said a small red stain, less than half a centimetre in diameter, was located on a bag found in the KitchenAid box.

Nielsen explained how officers used a Hemastix on the stain. By now the jury had heard a lot about these Hemastix tests, presumptive tests for blood.

Nielsen presented for the court and entered into evidence the KitchenAid box, the backpack, and the grocery bag. Then he unwrapped a very large bag of weed, telling the court it contained 14.63 pounds of marijuana that was in the box. That was followed by another 5.24 pounds of weed he said was found in the backpack and 1.03 pounds of marijuana found in the grocery bags.

On cross-examination, the defence asked Rotta-Loria why he was wearing nitrile gloves, the same gloves police wear to process crimes scenes, when he looked at those items. Rotta-Loria had taken a box from the lab for cleaning around the house.

"I watched a lot of crime shows," came the response. The PhD student surely never imagined he'd end up in the middle of a real-life crime scene.

Matthew Donovan testified he was Adam Sandeson's roommate. The twenty-one-year-old had just finished his fourth year of engineering at Dal. He told the court he and Adam Sandeson were teammates on the Dal men's volleyball team. He had met Will Sandeson a few times.

He recounted the same story as Rotta-Loria, telling the court about discovering the weed and Adam getting a call from his dad that his brother had been arrested for murder.

"Adam was obviously very upset," he told the jury. "I spent most of the night consoling him, spending time with him."

Adam Sandeson also testified in his brother's murder trial. He told the jury he got some texts from Will on August 17 between 7 and 8 A.M. saying he was coming by to drop off laundry, as he often did. Adam said he went to work and Will came by that evening. He told the court they just talked about "general stuff, nothing out of the ordinary."

Will was there for less than an hour. Adam didn't see him bring any laundry.

"He said something about something might smell a little in the basement," the younger Sandeson told the court.

When Will left, Adam went downstairs to see what he meant. That's when he saw an Adidas backpack with marijuana in it. He opened it but left it where it was and brought it up with Will the next day.

"I asked him about it, and he said it wasn't his, I think, and that there was more."

Adam Sandeson said he and his roommates went downstairs to confirm what Will had said and discovered the KitchenAid box.

"I think after we saw that down there, I learned a little more about what was going on."

He and his roommates had a chat about what to do.

As his brother testified William Sandeson was sitting in the courtroom, writing notes.

When the Crown completed its questioning, the defence team conferred with Will for a few minutes, before deciding not to cross-examine his brother.

CHAPTER 12
THE CROWN'S CASE: SEARCHING THE FARM

Don Calpito, senior security investigator with Telus Communications Company based in Toronto, told the court he's used primarily as a witness by Telus in criminal trials and helps police interpret phone records they obtain from his company.

Calpito brought maps with him to help the jury see where William Sandeson's phone was at specific times. He testified there was an outgoing call from Sandeson's phone on the morning of August 18 using a tower near Truro and Brookfield. The call lasted 189 seconds.

By 12:38 P.M., Sandeson, or at least his phone, was back in Halifax, pinging off a tower at Dalhousie University.

At 12:53 there was an outgoing call from Sandeson's phone near Ahern Manor at 2313 Gottingen Street. That call was twenty-seven seconds long. Halifax Police Headquarters is located at 1975 Gottingen Street. Sergeant Charla Keddy previously testified Sandeson arrived to speak with her just before 1 P.M. on the 18th.

Calpito also had information from Taylor Samson's phone records. Just in case there was still any doubt, he testified there were no text messages to or from Samson's phone after August 15, 2015, at 10:40 P.M. His phone last pinged in Halifax, from a tower at Dal, when he sent a text message at 10:25 P.M. to William Sandeson. Calpito testified the fact that there are no incoming messages means the phone must be off or in a no-service area.

The cellphone records showed Sandeson had been in the area near his parents' farm in Lower Truro. He had also texted his dad, "Think I will be home Tuesday to drop off junk from Halifax. Just not sorted yet."

It led to an expansive six-day search of the family farm and surrounding areas.

⌐ ☡ ☘

Detective Constable Jonathan Jefferies testified he was a member of the homicide unit and the scene coordinator for the search of the farm and surrounding areas. His role was to be a liaison between the investigative team and the search team. He was also responsible for relaying anything of value to the investigative team.

He arrived on August 25 around 11 A.M.

"Michael Sandeson was home, along with his son, and at that point I executed the warrant on him," Jefferies told the jury.

Approximately fifteen minutes later, he executed the warrant on Michael's mother, Ruth Sandeson. She also has a home on the property. Jefferies advised the family where officers would be and what they could expect over the coming days.

There were also farms on either side of the Sandeson farm, and Jefferies sent other officers to speak with those owners to obtain their consent to search their properties. They agreed.

Police had erected a command bus behind the main home. Ground Search and Rescue had its own command site, down the road at the fire hall.

Larry Corbin had been a volunteer with Ground Search and Rescue for ten years. When it came to the Sandeson case, he didn't exactly know what he was looking for.

"They told us we could possibly find human remains and then just to search the area and look for anything that doesn't look like it's supposed to be there," he told the court.

Combing through thick brush on the very large property, Corbin found a rusty-coloured pair of gloves, balled up, one folded inside the other.

"We were given the area to search right behind a farmhouse. There was a brook that ran up and basically when we come out of one little spot in the treeline, they were laying right there at the edge," he testified, detailing the difficult terrain.

The gloves looked like the ones William Sandeson is seen wearing in surveillance video outside his Halifax apartment.

Corbin notified the command post, flagged the area with orange tape, and continued on.

Corporal Shawn Reynolds was the Ground Search and Rescue incident commander. After trying to locate the site with the help of a GPS twice, he called on Corbin to lead him to the gloves. It was early afternoon.

"He led me down a little tiny trail where there's a bit of a valley, a bit of a depression in the ground with a number of old trucks, and there was a small footpath, down the footpath and to the left...he showed me a red pair of gloves that were in a ball."

Reynolds called Jefferies, who contacted Constable Sayer who eventually became the lead investigator. Sayer told him the gloves might be relevant to the investigation and tasked Jefferies with seizing them.

"I took the gloves, placed them into an exhibit bag, and sealed the bag right away," Jefferies testified. He turned the gloves over to the investigative triangle.

Later the same day, there was another find.

Wayne Burns had been a volunteer with Ground Search and Rescue for fifteen years. On August 27, he said he was told to keep an eye out for anything out of the ordinary. He got a call that a member of his team found some garbage bags and an Adidas bag in the bed of an old abandoned truck.

"I was the team leader so I was not very far away and I went up and I established it was something of interest and I called the command post."

He stayed until the RCMP arrived around forty-five minutes later.

The searchers would not have been aware but William Sandeson had been seen on video loading garbage bags and a blue Adidas bag into the trunk of his car the same morning his phone had pinged in the Truro area.

Corporal Reynolds walked down the same footpath with Wayne Burns in amongst those old trucks.

"It looks like a former ice-cream box on a five-tonne truck," he told the jury. Behind a door labelled number two, Burns showed Reynolds the bags he had found inside. Reynolds called other officers, who held the scene and seized the evidence.

There were between twenty-five and eighty people searching the property, depending on the day.

Detective Constable Illya Nielsen of the Ident Unit arrived at the farm around 9:13 P.M. the night the gloves were found. He had tested them for blood earlier in the day but that test came back negative. Nielsen was called back when the items were found inside the so-called ice-cream truck.

He went through a booklet of photos he took at the farm.

"You're looking at a dirt road on the east side of the field at the Sandeson farm, that leads down into a gully," he told the jury. "As you approach the other side of that little road, there's a little path through the bushes, and as you go down through the bushes, you can see there's the back of a bed of an old truck down in the gully."

Found inside a compartment in the truck was the blue Adidas bag and three garbage bags that would give the police even more evidence against William Sandeson.

Nielsen said there was some staining on the floor under the blue Adidas bag, so he did a swab and stored it in a Tyvek sleeve. He testified he was wearing protective booties as well as blue nitrile gloves while he searched this scene.

He said the items found in the truck were brought back to police headquarters in Halifax that night, where the contents were photographed.

The first photos were of the blue Adidas bag and its contents.

"There was a strong decomposing rotting smell coming from this bag," Nielsen testified.

There was a large black duffle bag located inside the blue Adidas bag.

"The duffle bag and the contents, there was towels, were extremely wet. They were soaked."

Nielsen explained the best way to preserve DNA is to dry items as quickly as possible, so the items were hung in drying cabinets.

He said there was a blue tarp inside the first garbage bag. Inside the second garbage bag, two yellow fibre cloths, a box for a bag of garbage bags, a grey microfibre cloth, an orange-and-black stained towel, a blue microfibre stained towel, a shower curtain, a shower-curtain ring, a stack of unused black garbage bags, and a soaked roll of paper towel.

"All these items were wet, soaking wet," Nielsen added.

"Were you able to tell with what?" McOnie asked.

"These orange stained cloths had a strong smell of cleaner that came from them, but the rest seemed to be soaked with water," he said.

Inside the third garbage bag located in that old truck, Nielsen found a roll of tinfoil, a plastic bag with a strange reddish-rusty-coloured substance inside, an empty container of blueberries, a balled-up piece of dry paper towel, an empty bag of cat litter, a can of Lysol disinfectant spray, peanut butter, and other packaging and household waste.

At 10 A.M. the next day, Nielsen went back to the farm again to take more photos in daylight.

Eleven and a half metres from the truck where the other items had been located, police found some garbage at the base of a tree. It included an envelope with the name "William" and a partial address "12 something" in Halifax, Nielsen testified, a Bank of

Montreal letter addressed to "William Sandeson," and a Dalhousie student planner.

Sergeant André Habib, also in the Forensic Unit, showed up at the farm that day. He told the jury he helped with the search, working alongside Ground Search and Rescue.

"That day I was primarily tasked with sifting through cow manure," he said. "There's a lot of cow manure on a farm and one of the cadaver dogs had indicated earlier that there was something there. They're trained to sit when they believe there's human remains there."

The next day, August 29, the cadaver dog had indicated there was something near a body of water, a small pond, near the family farm. Habib was part of the team that drained that pond so they could see the bottom.

"We enlisted the help of a local company that brought in pumps and that went on into the next day until finally that pond was cleared."

"What was it you were looking for?" Susan MacKay asked

"I was looking for a body," Habib said. It was blunt.

He never found what he was looking for.

On September 23, Jefferies went to the correctional centre to make a plea to Sandeson regarding the whereabouts of Samson's body. Jefferies testified Sandeson told him he didn't wish to speak to him about that.

CHAPTER 13
THE CROWN'S CASE: FORENSICS

Throughout the trial, the jury had heard a great deal about staining that looked like blood or that officers believed was blood. Now they would get to find out whether it actually was.

Detective Constable James Wasson was in his thirtieth year of service with Halifax Police. It was his job to decide which evidence would be sent to the RCMP's National Forensic Lab in Ottawa. Wasson testified he was on a day off, on August 19, 2015, when he got a call asking him to coordinate this file. He arrived at work at noon and had a look at the evidence that had been gathered so far. He did a walkthrough of the scene later that day, at 6:09 P.M.

Wasson also seized Sandeson's clothes and photographed an injury on his right shoulder. He testified there were areas of staining on the inner soles of both of his shoes. They reacted positively when officers used the presumptive test for blood. He sent one of the swabs to the lab but there wasn't enough for a DNA profile.

He also marked some areas on pants seized from Sandeson's apartment. They tested positive with the presumptive test for blood and were sent to the lab for further testing but they came back negative.

Wasson swabbed the handgun seized from a locked safe at 1210 Henry Street and treated it with cyanoacrylate, or Krazy Glue fumes.

"What happens is the Krazy Glue fumes will stick to the oils that are deposited from the hands to the gun in search for fingerprints," he told the jury.

"While I was processing the gun for fingerprints, I noticed various staining on here, red staining."

He swabbed multiple areas of the gun and sent them off to the lab. He also swabbed the mouth of Taylor Samson's water bottle and his razor, looking for Samson's DNA. Those swabs, along with DNA samples from Samson's mother and father, were also sent to the lab in an effort to create a DNA profile for him.

On cross-examination, Eugene Tan asked Wasson about checking the knives, an axe, and a sword found in Sandeson's apartment for blood. Wasson agreed that he did.

"Why would you have done that?" Tan probed

"In the event the body had been cut up," Wasson replied, before agreeing the results were all negative.

Wasson also testified he couldn't get any usable fingerprints from Sandeson's gun.

Tan asked why Wasson took a swab of the grip and trigger on the gun.

"I wanted to know who was holding the gun. That's typical function if you're holding and shooting a gun—you hold onto the grip, you pull the trigger, so those are the areas that I swabbed, basically looking for the user's DNA."

Florence Célestin, a forensic DNA specialist who works for the RCMP's forensic lab in Ottawa, was accepted by the court as a qualified expert to provide opinion evidence in the forensic interpretation of DNA profiles. She testified she's worked on approximately 740 different cases and testified as an expert witness 12 times in various courts across Canada.

"Do you acknowledge and accept that you have a duty even though you work for the RCMP, to give fair, objective, and non-partisan opinion evidence?" asked Susan MacKay.

"That is correct," Célestin agreed.

She explained how her team tests exhibits when they arrive at the lab in Ottawa. She said DNA technologists go through a four-step process to obtain a DNA profile, the first of which is extraction of the DNA.

"The DNA is in most of the cells of our body. For example if you have a peach, and you have a pit of a peach, the cell is like the peach, the pit of the peach would be the nucleus of the cell and inside it would be where the DNA is," she explained. "So part of that extraction process is to break that nucleus open to get the DNA."

The second step is quantification, to determine how much DNA is present. Célestin told the court the ideal amount to obtain a quality DNA profile is one nanogram, but they can do it with less.

The third step is amplification, making copies of the very specific regions of the DNA that they use in forensic science.

"Ninety-nine per cent of our DNA, or even 99.9, is the same," she elaborated. "That's why we all have, if all works well, two arms, one head, one heart, that's how we're made. There's this .01 per cent of the DNA that varies among individuals, and that's what we use in forensic science to help differentiate between two individuals."

The fourth and final step is to visualize the DNA profile using specialized software.

That's when a specialist like Célestin gets involved to do the interpretation.

"All right," said Susan MacKay. "Do any of the DNA samples or do any of the major contributors of the DNA samples from the different scenes and objects submitted in relation to this case, match the DNA that you are attributing to Taylor Samson?"

"Yes," replied Célestin.

She explained to the jury that generally she works with known DNA samples from alleged complainants or victims. In this case that was not possible as Taylor Samson's remains still hadn't been located, so Célestin told the jury police provided the "next best thing," a "quasi known" or a "putative known" sample. Those samples come from personal effects. In this case, the lab received the swaths from Samson's water bottle and razor. It worked. The lab obtained a profile. To have more assurance that it was correct, they compared the profile against the DNA of Samson's parents. She explained that we inherit DNA from our parents.

"Basically, it is 91 billion times more likely that this DNA profile is the child of the two parents rather than someone else unrelated. So 91 billion times more likely is a very strong support for parentage. When you have over ten thousand, it's a very strong support for parentage."

From that point on, the lab proceeded with the belief they were working with Samson's DNA.

Célestin testified swabs from the bathroom and the table at the Henry Street apartment matched Taylor Samson's DNA. Samson's DNA was also found on three pieces of flooring from the kitchen, on the frame of the entry door, on the chair in the kitchen, the heater in the kitchen, and the bullet found in the window casing.

Célestin told the jury Samson's DNA was also found on the swath of carpet torn from the trunk of Sandeson's car, on the tarp seized from the Sandeson farm, on the shower curtain also found on the farm, and inside the duffle bag William Sandeson told police was the biggest bag he'd ever seen.

She testified there were two DNA matches on the gun seized from the Henry Street apartment: Taylor Samson's and William Sandeson's.

Susan MacKay then asked Célestin to comment on another report from her lab that showed blood was not confirmed on the gun. She explained that it was a different swab, from a different area of the gun, that showed the presence of Samson's DNA.

Célestin referred to some areas of her report that said "blood identified," for example, on the kitchen table and chair, in the bathroom, the flooring, in the trunk, on the tarp and in the duffle bag.

"Blood identified means that the confirmatory test for blood was positive, so we know for a fact that it is blood. We don't know if it's human or animal at this point, but once we obtain a human DNA profile, then we know it is human blood."

Célestin said with regard to the sample from money found in Sandeson's apartment, it tested positive for blood, but did not meet the minimum requirement of 0.25 nanograms required for DNA processing. (Today that minimum threshold is 0.15.)

The Crown completed its questioning by asking if there were any concerns about contamination at the lab in Ottawa. The witness said not that she was aware of.

And that's exactly where Eugene Tan picked up his cross-examination.

"In fact, at least one exhibit arrived at the lab in a plastic bag that had been perforated, is that correct?"

"I don't recall. I would have to check the file."

Tan referred the witness to page 424 of the file.

"Yes, one of the exhibits had some minor damage, described as small tears," Célestin finally agreed, noting it was the pieces of flooring.

"So does that raise any issues of contamination or cross-contamination?" Tan continued.

Célestin replied that it would depend on what other exhibits it was packaged with, but if the bag was placed inside a box on its own, there would be no contamination.

"In fact, there was another occasion in which there was a spill by one of the technicians," Tan pressed on.

The witness looked up the page in the file once again, telling the court the technologist reported the edge of the plate she was using got caught on her lab coat. But Célestin said there are procedures in place to deal with this kind of thing, and there was no contamination.

And as much as Susan MacKay highlighted the areas in the lab's reports where blood was found, Tan wanted to know more about the areas where blood was not found, pointing out the confirmatory tests for blood on Sandeson's pants were negative, and there was not enough DNA discovered for processing. Célestin explained that blood may still be present even if it can't be confirmed.

Tan asked Célestin about her testimony that presumptive tests for blood could give a false positive in the presence of metal. He wanted to know how the reading would be affected if the sample itself was being collected off a metal surface.

Célestin agreed there could be false positives in the presence of metal, rust, bleach, and leather, but that's why it's only a screening test.

"But that has no impact on the DNA that's present on the sample," she said.

On that point, it seemed there could be no arguing.

The Crown's next witness was the RCMP's Sergeant Adrian Butler. He's one of seven bloodstain pattern analysts for the RCMP in Canada and was also qualified as an expert in this trial.

"It's the examination of the size, shape, location, distribution, and number of bloodstains in order to provide an interpretation of the physical events that gave rise to their origin," Butler explained, reading from a presentation he prepared to help the jury understand his role.

"Basically, I go to the scene or look at exhibits and try to determine what happened."

Butler said bloodstain patterns are predictable.

"When blood leaves the body, its behaviour will follow the laws of the physical sciences. It is not affected by age, sex, body temperature, alcohol content, or disease process."

He told the court he can determine the distance between where the blood is and where it originated, whether the mechanism used was a baseball bat or a gun, the position of the victim and the assailant during the blood shedding, and perhaps the minimum number of blows.

"We might be able to confirm or refute statements of witnesses or the accused," he continued, also explaining the basic bloodstain categories: passive, spatter, and transfer.

Passive refers to bloodstain patterns that are formed primarily from gravity, like when a single drop of blood falls to a surface. A drip trail, he said, is a source of blood travelling between two points. A drip pattern is a liquid dripping into another liquid, at least one of those liquids being blood. Pooling is an accumulation of blood on a surface, and a splash pattern is a volume of blood that falls or spills onto a surface.

Spatter bloodstain patterns include impact patterns, where an object strikes liquid blood. A cast-off pattern is where there is blood on an object and as the object is swung the blood is released from the object due to motion. An expired pattern is produced by blood that is forced by airflow out of the nose, mouth, or wound. Forward spatter is created by a projectile fired from a gun going in one direction and creating spatter that goes in the same direction as the projectile, and back spatter goes in the opposite direction to the force applied, like when a firearm is fired and the blood goes in the reverse direction. Arterial pattern is created when a major artery or vein is breached, creating blood that's projected under pressure, and satellite spatter is created when blood striking a surface as a drop of blood drops creates secondary spatter.

Transfer bloodstains result from contact between a blood-bearing object and another surface. Among them are saturation stains, resulting from the accumulation of liquid blood in an absorbent material; swipe patterns, resulting from the transfer of blood from a blood-bearing surface onto another surface with characteristics that indicate relative motion between the two surfaces; wipe patterns, resulting when altered bloodstain patterns result from an object moving through a pre-existing wet bloodstain.

Butler said he was asked to look at photos of the gun in this case and prepared a report.

"Perhaps you could just cut to the chase and tell us about that," said MacKay. "What did you find in regard to the gun you examined?"

"There was a minimum of forty-four spatter stains less than one millimetre in size located on the left side of the handgun slide," Butler replied, showing the jury photographs.

"The higher the energy or force, the smaller the stains you'll find," he testified, explaining that a foot landing in a pool of blood would create larger stains than a baseball bat.

"What about in the example of a gun being shot?" MacKay asked.

"A gun being shot you would have misting stains, which would be more like a paint spray can."

Butler also testified there were a minimum of four spatter stains, also less than one millimetre in size, located on the muzzle of the pistol.

"The fact that there is spatter stains, or what I believe to be spatter stains, on the muzzle of the gun, means that it was in close proximity to the blood source."

He testified there were a minimum of seven spatter stains, also tiny, on the right side of the handgun slide.

"What is your opinion as to what type of stain we're seeing on this gun?" MacKay asked.

Butler said this is a case of back spatter, mostly because the stains were all very small and on three sides of the gun. He told the jury that means the gun was between two and four feet from the source.

"It's my opinion that it's somewhat closer than four feet, but definitely within four feet," he testified.

It was time for cross-examination.

"Sergeant, in preparing your report there are a number of assumptions that you have made, is that correct?" Eugene Tan began.

"That's correct," agreed the officer.

Tan said first and foremost, Butler had assumed the gun had tested positive for blood. Butler agreed that he had, based on the DNA analysis already before the court. Tan produced the report and pointed out some of the areas Butler assumed to be blood showed, "blood not confirmed."

"'Blood not confirmed' doesn't mean there wasn't a presumptive test done for blood," Butler finished.

"Right, but you have not been qualified in the area of DNA analysis, have you?"

"No, but it's not saying that it's not blood," Butler persisted.

Tan wanted to know if the DNA report had any impact on Butler's analysis. He said it did not.

"I still believe that what's on the gun is blood," Butler said.

"You've also made an assumption that the pattern that you've noticed is a result of back spatter. Correct?"

"That's correct."

"Okay, let's talk about the difference between back spatter and forward spatter." Tan's questions were coming fast and furious. "Back spatter being a high energy force being applied to a form of blood and then it comes back to the source of the energy, right?"

"That's correct."

"And in the case of forward spatter it would be the projection of the blood in the same direction essentially as the application of force."

"That's correct."

"But you can't tell from what you've seen whether this is back spatter or forward spatter, can you?"

"If you're going to have forward spatter, you would have a lot more. You could have possible biological material, pieces of bone, skull. You wouldn't just have fine spatter."

"And that would be at the point immediately after the matter had struck the weapon. Is that correct?"

"That's correct."

"What if I were to say to you that this weapon was not seized until the afternoon or evening of August nineteenth?" Tan asked, pointing out that was three and a half to four days after it was allegedly fired.

"I can't see how it would have any relevance."

Tan pointed out that it wasn't in an evidence bag during that time and no one knows who may have handled it.

"I just looked at the photographs of the gun," Butler relented.

Tan provided Butler pictures of Sandeson's kitchen.

"Let's assume for a moment that somebody is sitting in that chair on the far left. In the event that that person is shot from behind with a nine-millimetre projectile. You would expect forward spatter. Correct?"

"It's possible," Butler testified, maintaining that scenario could also produce back spatter.

The Crown's next witness would have much more to say about the gun.

Laura Knowles, the firearms section team leader at the RCMP's National Forensic Laboratory, was qualified to testify at this trial as a firearms expert via video link from Ottawa.

Knowles told the court she received three exhibits in relation to the firearms and toolmark evidence in this case, a Smith & Wesson pistol, one fired bullet, and one cartridge. She examined them and provided a report. Knowles found the gun was capable of discharge and that it had a trigger pull weight of seven pounds, meaning how much it takes to pull the trigger. She said seven pounds is pretty typical.

"To give you an idea of what seven pounds feels like, if you've ever opened a Coke can, pulling that tab with your finger, that feels like about five pounds."

She testified the gun did not discharge through the shock-discharge test, a test to see whether the gun is capable of discharge without pulling the trigger, and that it is a restricted weapon but not a prohibited weapon.

Knowles said she fired bullets from Sandeson's gun so she could compare them to the fired bullet she was provided. She found the fired bullet had similar class characteristics, for example the calibre, to the firearm in question, but she could not definitively say whether or not it was fired from that gun.

"It means that there was not enough individual character on the bullet in agreement with the test fires that I fired from the firearm," she told the court, explaining that was because of the condition of the bullet.

"To the naked eye it looked very pristine, but from a microscopic level, it had a lot of damage on its surface. Often we find that this is the case if a bullet goes through something post discharge like a window or a wall." The bullet she examined was found in the window frame in Sandeson's apartment.

When it came to the cartridge, which is a full round of unfired ammunition, she concluded that it had been chambered, cycled through, or otherwise in contact with the pistol, meaning someone had loaded the cartridge in that gun and fired one round.

On cross-examination Eugene Tan asked Knowles if it were true that the only thing she could confidently say about the bullet was that it could have been fired from any gun with similar characteristics. She agreed.

CHAPTER 14

THE CROWN'S CASE: MOTIVE FOR MURDER

Crown Attorney Kim McOnie was quick to tell the jury that the Crown did not have to prove motive, that she and her colleague had no responsibility to prove why William Sandeson killed Taylor Samson. But that didn't stop her from arguing there was motive and laying out the evidence to show that motive was greed and financial gain.

It had already been established that there was to be a drug deal for $40,000, but the Crown told the jury the actual street value of the drugs was $90,000. They were later told to disregard the street value because the Crown failed to present evidence on that fact, but the seed had been planted.

The Crown then set about establishing just how badly Sandeson needed that cash. Kim McOnie called Adam Hayden, the branch manager for the CIBC in Truro, to the stand. He told the court William Sandeson had a $200,000 professional-student line of credit with his bank that was opened in July 2013. A letter from Saba University, where Sandeson completed a semester of medical school, was attached to the file.

"We used that to verify that the individual would be attending medical school," Hayden explained. During his first statement to police, when he was still a witness, Sandeson told the officer he had hated his time at Saba and that it had "soared his debt." However, on cross-examination, Hayden conceded that while the account was opened as a professional-student line of credit there was no requirement for Sandeson to confirm what the money was going to be used for upon withdrawal.

He also explained that meant Sandeson had $200,000 at his fingertips. His mother co-signed for the loan and had authority to deal with the account. The statements were sent to the Sandeson family farm in Lower Truro.

The recent statements were read into the record and copies provided for the jury. On July 9, 2015, the balance was $73,723.85, meaning that's how much Sandeson already owed on the account. During that month, some payments were made, including a $1,000 e-transfer from his girlfriend, Sonja. On July 14, there was an internet transfer withdrawing $3,000 from the account and on July 17, $500 was withdrawn from a bank machine in Lower Sackville. On July 20, another $500 was withdrawn, this time from a bank machine on Girouard Street. A couple of payments were credited to the account but always less than the withdrawals. On July 29 there was an e-transfer of another $3,000, followed by another two on August 10 of $800 and $1,500 respectively. As of the end of the statement period on September 9, William Sandeson owed $78,518.59 and he hadn't even started Dal medical school yet.

The jury was also provided with a series of text messages between Sandeson and three different people, all of which the Crown argued illustrated he was under financial stress.

RCMP forensic analyst Gilles Marchand, whose job it was to recover and preserve data from electronic devices associated with the case, testified he analyzed three cellphones, all of which were iPhones. It was unclear whether Sandeson owned all three but

Taylor Samson's phone was never found. Marchand told the jury he was able to extract call logs, contacts, text messages, chat information, photos, and videos, all of which he provided to investigators. He said he was given a password to access the phone from another officer, who presumably got it from Sandeson himself. Marchand said he has now figured out how to access phones without the password, but at the time he would not have been able to do it, had it not been provided to him.

Marchand created a series of reports based on Sandeson's text history. They were all provided to the jury; however only selections were read aloud in court.

On May 3, 2015, at 8:40 P.M., Sandeson texted his mother, Laurie Sandeson, asking, "How much money is left in the RESP?"

She didn't respond until 11:38 the next morning: "I'd have to check William."

He responded the day after that, on May 5 at 1:45 P.M., "Could you please check."

Right away his mom said, "Should have a statement at home. I'll check this evening."

William continued the conversation ten minutes after that, "Thank you! I made stock investments today though CIBC as well." And before she could respond, "Using a TFSA."

"I just had a call from James, CIBC, and he said that he met you," Laurie Sandeson texted back. "'What a fine young gentleman' he told me." And then she addressed her son's other message, "Stocks eh? I was never quite brave enough to invest in those. Did you go with local ones such as NS Power, Emera Group, (Sobeys)"

"I went mostly with international corporations, Canadian banks, and United States business like apple and Microsoft," her son responded. "Very diversified with some money dedicated to bonds as well," he continued.

"Sounds fairly safe," his mom texted. "Apple is now the largest company in the world with billions of dollars in profit last year alone."

"I'm not surprised by that. They've developed so many products which dominate their respective markets," Sandeson said, and that was the end of the conversation between mother and son for now.

The next day at 2:16 P.M. Laurie Sandeson got in touch again. "I have a call in to Gerry Rau at CIBC regarding our resp account. Will let you know status when I hear back. Sounds like you are looking for some financial assistance??"

In between idle chatter about whether he'd be home soon because his younger brother wanted to borrow his leather jacket for his high school's production of the musical, *Grease*, Will said, "I was expecting a much larger tax return."

A while later, his mom said, "Just heard back from Gerry at CIBC, and yes, there's a few dollars there which you can access—how much were you hoping for?"

"I was just expecting a tax return of $1,000," Sandeson replied fifteen minutes later.

It was not until the following morning that the sporadic texting about money continued. "I believe you need to provide proof of enrollment to cibc in order to enable withdrawal of funds from RESP," Laurie told her son. "How about a $2–3000 withdrawal?"

"How is there that much left?" Will texted back.

"We have just one RESP account but we tried to divvy the amount up per child," his mom explained. "You didn't draw much from it during your 3 year degree program and Adam has dipped in twice now. Matthew has his own Knowledge First Fund and we want to save something for David. We can talk more when you come home later this week."

"Save it, I'm fine without it," said William.

But his mother wasn't quite ready to let it go, "We'll chat."

If they did chat, they didn't do it over text. Sandeson did, however, text his father, Michael Sandeson, about his money woes more than two months later. On July 17 at 1:41 P.M., Sandeson received a text from his dad: "Laurie got mail today. She is mad over credit line."

"Well she has no need to be," Sandeson replied, and before his father could respond, "Will be paid this September."

The morning after Taylor Samson disappeared, Sandeson received another text from his dad: "Coming to Hlfx to fix Adams door. Anything you want? Have truck."

It was yet another indication of just how typical this family was.

"I don't need anything thanks," Sandeson texted back at 10:53 A.M. on August 16.

"Think I will be home Tuesday to drop off junk from Halifax. Just not sorted yet," Sandeson continued. He did go home that Tuesday morning, and the evidence indicated he had indeed dropped off "junk."

But before he did that, on Monday, August 17, at 6:16 in the evening, William Sandeson texted his father, "Just approved for student grant of 7000!"

"Weehooo," his dad exclaimed. Clearly, he had no idea what his son had been up to.

In her closing argument Crown Attorney Kim McOnie also referred to messages between William Sandeson and Jordan MacEwan, an associate of both Sandeson and Samson. He had been the subject of a break-in two nights before Samson was killed.

In the midst of a conversation about Taylor's disappearance, Sandeson wrote to MacEwan, "Splitting debt with him and said I'd have the money by Christmas. So I need 20k by Christmas. Fuck," and later, "I think I can make good on my other product. Can get keys for 19. Worse comes to worse, I take out a loan."

"So in the Crown's submission, there's certainly evidence that's before you that Mr. Sandeson was strapped for cash," argued Kim McOnie to the court. "He's asking his mother about making withdrawals from the RESP account, he's telling his father that he will pay the line of credit off by September, and he's telling Jordan that he owes some guy twenty thousand by December."

She went on to point out Sandeson was about to start medical school, was maintaining an apartment in the city, and maintaining three vehicles: a motorcycle, a truck, and a car.

"So in the Crown's submission he's under a significant amount of financial pressure," she continued, reminding the jury Sandeson had told people he was planning to get out of the drug-dealing business with the transaction with Taylor that night. "So we say, to clear off some or all of that debt, the deal had to be a big one, and it was," McOnie underlined.

⌐ ℞ ☘

While the defence argued at length about how incoherent and panicked Sandeson was the night of August 15, 2015, the Crown argued he was actually giddy, as evidenced by text messages with another friend, Amanda Clarke.

Her name came up several times during the court proceedings and while text history indicates she knew Sandeson's parents, the extent of their relationship is also unclear. On August 16 at 1:42 A.M., only hours after Samson was seen walking into Sandeson's apartment, Sandeson texted Clarke, "Have a little catch-up tomorrow?"

At 4:53 A.M., she responded, "Potentially! I have to get a medical done tomorrow morning for my Aussie visa, then I'll message you! If not, then Tuesday morning works for me."

At 4:59 Sandeson asked, "Have a chance to [Snapchat]?" but three minutes later before Amanda Clarke could respond, he texted again, "Student loan paid off and I'm completely squeaky clean now! Sold market share away."

It was six and a half hours after Taylor Samson was last seen alive.

"Do those text messages to Amanda give the impression of someone who was in a panic? Of someone who's incoherent?" Kim McOnie asked rhetorically, declaring the messages actually portrayed a tone of excitement. "He paid off his student loan!" she repeated. "He's squeaky clean. That is what we say this was all about"—she paused for emphasis—"*money*."

McOnie argued the big black duffle bag Taylor Samson was seen on video carrying into Sandeson's apartment was taken out during the time the DVR system was turned off and Samson's body, or parts of it, was inside it.

"This is not a Hollywood film where masked invaders or Morphsuited intruders bust in through a window, shoot someone, and take the money with them," she said. "This is reality, a reality where every shred of physical evidence [...] points to one person as being responsible for the death of Mr. Samson."

She asked the jury to find William Sandeson guilty.

CHAPTER 15
IN HIS OWN DEFENCE

By now speculation was swirling in Halifax about whether William Sandeson would take the stand in his own defence. People wanted to hear what he had to say, but they would have to wait a little longer to find out whether they would get that opportunity.

The defence decided to forego its opportunity to present an opening address, proceeding straight to the evidence. It was June 5, 2017.

Jordan MacEwan, twenty-four, told the court he was employed by a temp agency, usually working at Scotiabank Centre setting up events, though he had only been doing that for a few months.

"Mr. MacEwan, I want to ask you, do you know William Sandeson?" Tan asked.

"Yes, I do."

"And how is it that you know William Sandeson?"

"I met him through selling weed."

MacEwan testified he met Sandeson about three years before.

"Somebody told him that I sold weed and he needed some," he told the jury.

Tan asked if MacEwan also knew Taylor Samson. MacEwan said that he met him in the beginning of the summer of 2015, the same way he met William Sandeson.

Tan asked MacEwan what he remembered about August 13, 2015.

"Are you talking about the night I got house invaded?" MacEwan asked.

He was.

MacEwan said he was in contact with Taylor Samson that day because Samson owed him money, mostly for mushrooms and a little bit of weed. It was around $1,500 and Samson had owed him the money for a couple of weeks. "He was just going to come by and drop money off, around ten probably, I would say."

MacEwan testified he waited around for Samson until around 2 A.M. but got tired of waiting, gave up, and went to sleep.

"I can't remember exactly the thirty minutes around there because I was smoking weed the whole time waiting for him. I smoked a fair amount."

MacEwan told the court Samson said he was going to throw the money through the window of his apartment. He thought, perhaps, he got around $700, roughly half of what he was owed, but couldn't really remember.

"I went to sleep and about thirty or so after I went to sleep, I was woken up to a light being turned on to an unfamiliar face and that guy jumping on top of me and started to beat me."

MacEwan said there were three guys in total, two dark skinned and one lighter skinned.

"Two guys were running around looking for stuff in the house, and one guy was on top of me fighting me."

MacEwan said he was in bed, but he tried to get up on his knees.

"They were just sitting there just punching me in the face, and I was kind of like, 'What do I do? What do I do, right?' Like, I don't know what to do here. Then one guy yells, 'Tie him up. We know you have more stuff here.'"

MacEwan said the men found weed and mushrooms.

He said he was being beaten with police batons.

"What did you believe that they were looking for?" Tan asked.

"Money and drugs," MacEwan replied.

Money and drugs. The two simple ingredients of this ever-so-complex case.

MacEwan said in addition to the pound of weed and half a pound of mushrooms, he had about $10,000 hidden in his apartment.

He tried to fight back, he testified, but there was no use.

"Two of them start hitting me and then one of them puts me in a chokehold and then I'm just looking around, thinking like, 'I'm screwed.' You know what I mean? And then I get to my wall and push off my wall and we fly over my bed. I get out of the chokehold. Then, that's when a police baton hits me right in the face, right on the temple."

He managed to grab the police baton and hit one of the guys two or three times, getting away and running for the door, but one of the guys caught up to him and tackled him down the stairs outside.

"I was yelling, 'Help!' as soon as I got outside, like screaming it. And then when I went to turn around, they were running up my driveway. Gone."

But MacEwan's dramatic tale wasn't over. He just kept talking.

"I was naked the whole fight too, covered in blood," he continued. "I was pretty much blacking out at this point, from, I assume, lack of blood."

He told the court the intruders took the pound of weed and half a pound of mushrooms, but nothing more.

"Mr. MacEwan, did the police ever get involved with this altercation?"

"No, I didn't call the cops about it."

"All right. Why not?"

"Because I wanted to continue selling. I didn't want them involved with it."

MacEwan said he did eventually tell police this story when he was brought in by detectives regarding the Samson case. He couldn't remember how much he told them. He did remember the officers didn't go inside his apartment to look around. He said he had marks on him from the fight for about two weeks afterward, so the police would have seen them.

The Sandeson trial did not reveal who attacked Jordan MacEwan, investigators saying only that they determined it wasn't related to their case. It was investigated separately but no charges were ever laid.

"Do you recall if there was any specific questions that they would have asked you about the drugs that you would have had in your home?"

"I don't think they asked too much about that."

"Had you mentioned that you were expecting either payment or contact from Taylor Samson on the evening of the thirteenth?"

"I don't know, I'm not sure."

Tan switched the focus to MacEwan's relationship with Sandeson, whom he had known longer than Samson.

MacEwan told the court he borrowed money from Sandeson near the end of 2014, only a month or so after the two had met.

"How much was it that you borrowed from Mr. Sandeson?" Tan questioned.

"Fifteen thousand."

"And what was the purpose of that loan?"

"To get a big order of weed for a better price."

"Over what time period was it expected that you would repay him?"

"Every few months I would pay interest. It took me almost a year to pay it back and I ended up paying five or more thousand in interest."

"Did you feel pressure to make payments?

"Not at all. He didn't really give me any deadline."

Tan was trying to make the point that Sandeson didn't need money, as the Crown had alleged.

"Have you faced any criminal charges as a result of your involvement with drugs?" Tan asked.

MacEwan said he faced three trafficking charges. He said he was no longer in the drug trade.

"Why not?"

"Because I'm already in trouble."

When the Crown called Detective Constable Roger Sayer in reply evidence, he told the jury that in addition to collecting evidence to figure out what happened, police also collect evidence to determine what did not happen. Sayer referenced one of the several versions of events provided by William Sandeson in which he told his colleagues he was tired because he had a friend who had been attacked and he was up late helping him and he wasn't feeling well due to the strong smell of bleach. Jordan MacEwan never mentioned Sandeson helping him clean up the night he was attacked. Sayer testified the stories provided by Sandeson and MacEwan were "eerily similar" but by then police had received several different accounts from Sandeson and officers were weighing those accounts.

On cross-examination, Kim McOnie had MacEwan reiterate that he was pretty intoxicated on the night he described.

"Do you recall telling the police when you were interviewed that you didn't think Taylor had anything to do with this?"

"Yes."

"Do you recall telling police that you knew Will and Taylor had what you called a 'big deal' together?"

"I don't but I probably did say that."

"Do you recall telling police that Will had messaged you to say that Taylor had taken his money?"

"Yeah," he replied, but in such a hesitating way that it was clear he was not sure.

"When was it that you were finally able to pay off that loan that you had to Mr. Sandeson?"

"It was a while after all this happened. I ended up meeting his brother and giving him money. I think it was probably honestly over six months after that."

"How come you didn't pay it back to Mr. Sandeson himself?" McOnie asked.

"He was in jail at the time."

Kim McOnie had made a mistake. Justice Arnold wasn't pleased the jury was now aware William Sandeson was in custody. Some may have assumed he was behind bars because he was charged with murder, but the court had made significant efforts to ensure the jury never saw Sandeson in handcuffs, taking the time to bring him in and out of the courtroom when the jury was not present, in order to protect his right to be presumed innocent.

"You knew what that answer was before you asked him that question," Arnold told the Crown. "That wasn't a surprise. So what's the relevance of that question and answer?"

McOnie tried to explain that she was trying to get to the time frame of when the money was paid back, but Arnold persisted that that could have been done without asking why it wasn't paid directly to Sandeson.

"They have not seen Mr. Sandeson coming in and out of court in custody. We've taken great pains many times a day to avoid them seeing that or hearing about that. So why did the Crown elicit it during cross-examination during the defence case, is my question?"

Kim McOnie tried to explain that she knew MacEwan hadn't paid the money back within six months because he had previously testified otherwise.

"What did you think he was going to say? Did you think he was going to say anything other than Mr. Sandeson was in jail?"

McOnie agreed she should have phrased the question differently.

In the end the court agreed the defence would enter an admission, opting to take their chances that it was better for the jury to know why Sandeson was in custody, rather than speculating.

They didn't want the jury to think Sandeson may have committed another crime that also landed him in jail.

"The defence admits that William Sandeson has been in custody since the date of his arrest of August 18, 2015, in relation to this matter only and not in relation to any other matter," Sarson told the jury.

Arnold explained to the jury that the fact that a person charged with an offence is in custody during or prior to a trial has absolutely nothing to do with the decision they were about to make.

"It's just not relevant to this trial," he underscored.

After yet another complication, the trial continued.

The defence called its next witness, Sergeant Kim Robinson, a patrol supervisor with HRP. In August 2015, she was a detective constable in Major Crime and the lead investigator in this case for two months until she was promoted.

Robinson's testimony was very repetitive of what the trial had already heard. She reiterated much of what her colleagues had already told the jury, describing how the investigative triangle works, how the last call from Samson's phone was traced to the group home in Lower Sackville where Sandeson worked, and how Sandeson made plans to go to police headquarters to speak with officers.

Robinson testified she was watching parts of Sandeson's interview from another room with the investigative triangle, again reiterating how he allowed police to read and photograph his texts with Samson, how the messages were inconsistent with the information he had provided to police, and how that ultimately led to concern.

"We were shocked, I guess, is the best way to put it," Robinson stated. "This was not what we were expecting. My understanding was that he was a friend of his who had come in to speak with police and from what we were seeing at that point in time, he became a suspect."

Brad Sarson asked Robinson about the timing of police entering Sandeson's apartment before they had a search warrant.

Robinson told the jury police believed Samson had been abducted: "We believed his life was in danger, and it was our duty to protect his life."

Detective Constable Josh Underwood told the court he was detailed by Major Crime to find Jordan MacEwan and talk to him on the evening of August 18.

"There was some indication he had some knowledge of drug trafficking of the victim," Underwood told the court.

He said MacEwan had a black eye, and the door of his apartment looked like it had been forced open. Underwood said he told MacEwan he was investigating the disappearance of Taylor Samson. MacEwan told him about people breaking into his apartment and giving him the black eye and agreed to go to police headquarters to give a statement.

Sarson wanted to know what MacEwan told Underwood about any contact with Samson a few days prior to his disappearance.

"I think they had messaged back and forth and he told me Taylor had shown up and delivered some money to him."

"What explanation, if any, did Mr. MacEwan give you as to why Taylor gave him money?"

"He owed him money for drugs."

"And what, if any, information did Mr. MacEwan give you with respect to the timing as to when Mr. Samson gave him money versus when Mr. MacEwan's residence was broken into."

"It was the same night."

"Was there any more degree of specificity given than that?"

"If I recall correctly, it was about an hour after Taylor had delivered the money that Mr. MacEwan's apartment was broken into."

Sarson took a moment to confer with his client and co-counsel, before finishing with Detective Constable Underwood.

"Do you recall Mr. MacEwan also saying that he didn't think Taylor had anything to do with the home invasion?" Kim McOnie questioned on cross-examination.

"I do remember him saying that."

SANDESON'S GIRLFRIEND TAKES THE STAND

The defence called its final witness, Sonja Gashus, William Sandeson's girlfriend when Samson disappeared. Gashus, now twenty-three, told the jury she had just graduated with a bachelor of commerce from Dalhousie University. She now audited hedge funds. Gashus testified she was in a relationship with Sandeson beginning in January 2015.

"If we weren't at work or at track or at school, we were together usually," she said.

Sandeson sat, taking notes, as he did throughout the trial, while Gashus testified, looking up at her from time to time.

Gashus said on August 15, 2015, she was at Lawrencetown Beach with her friends. She went back to Sandeson's apartment on Henry Street around late afternoon. She didn't remember who was home, but recalled they went to the Stubborn Goat together for dinner.

"Did you notice anything in particular about the state of the apartment on August fifteenth?" Tan asked.

"It was cleaner than normal. I didn't notice it was messy and I usually would."

While the couple was at dinner, Gashus testified, Sandeson asked her not to be home [at his apartment] later that evening.

"Had Mr. Sandeson, in the past, asked you to be out of the apartment for any periods of time?"

"No."

Gashus told the court she did go back to the apartment for around an hour. She testified Sandeson was organizing the apartment, trying to remove certificates and anything that had his name on it. She couldn't recall what time she left the apartment, but said it was dark outside when she went to her friend's place nearby. She said there was no clear time frame as to when she should return but Sandeson told her he hoped it wouldn't be too long.

"You were sort of respecting Mr. Sandeson, saying that you would stay out of the apartment for a period of time. Is it possible that you could have returned at any time?"

"Yes."

Tan was making sure the jury knew Sandeson would have been taking a risk to plot a murder when his girlfriend could walk in the door at any moment.

As it was, she got the go-ahead to go back to Sandeson's apartment around 12:30 A.M. and said she left within five minutes.

Tan asked if she had any observations about the apartment itself when she returned.

"It smelled like cleaning products," Gashus replied.

She testified she went to bed as soon as she got there. She had to work at Starbucks at 6 A.M. Sandeson drove her to work and they left around 5:45 and picked up her co-worker along the way.

"Do you remember if Mr. Sandeson was dressed unusually?" Gashus's co-worker had previously testified he was dressed warmly for the weather.

"I didn't think so."

Gashus testified he was wearing a toque and a sweater.

"He would wear weird sweaters a lot," she laughed. "And he really liked that hat too."

Tan asked Gashus about the shower curtain in the bathroom at Will's place.

"It was grimy, mildew," she testified, adding she didn't know how long it had been there.

Tan asked if she was aware of any illegal activity by Sandeson. She testified that she was. She knew he sold marijuana.

"Was it ever done in your presence?"

"Yes."

"Okay, how frequently?"

"Maybe a total of twenty times."

She told the court she didn't like his involvement in the drug trade, and regularly told him that, especially when he was accepted into med school in March 2015.

"The evening of August 15, Mr. Sandeson asked you to leave, did you have a belief as to what was going to happen?"

"Yeah, I believed that it was him making a deal, and he said that he was gonna get out of the whole thing."

Gashus told the court she had ended her relationship with William Sandeson and had been in a new relationship for the past ten months.

It was the Crown's turn to question William Sandeson's girlfriend.

"What was it that Will Sandeson told you about what had happened that night at the apartment? The night of Saturday, August 15, 2015," Susan MacKay asked.

"He said that someone was beat up and they walked out and he was left to clean up the blood that was left."

"And you told the police how many people had been there, correct? He had said how many people had been there?"

"It was three, I believe."

He had first told police there were three people, then changed his story to two. Nothing added up.

"And what had he told you about what was going on at the apartment that night. Why were they there?"

"He had said to me that he was making a deal, so that he could get out of the whole drug-dealing situation."

"Okay, so what did he say about what had happened, about what had led up to this guy getting beaten up?"

"I didn't know what led up to it."

"Let's start with the guy who got beat up. What did he say about what happened to him?"

"That he got sucker-punched, for lack of a better word. That was about it. I didn't know anything about that person or what had exactly happened."

Gashus was having trouble recalling what exactly she had told police that night, so the Crown asked her to review her statement from August 19.

"And you had told the police, hadn't you, that the guy who beat the guy up paid Will in weed? And that it was in a box, and you motioned to the police, the size of the box. Is that correct?"

"I don't remember."

The Crown asked Gashus to review a transcript of her statement to police on August 19 to help with her memory. Gashus then said she assumed the transaction was in weed.

"I was concerned and I asked, 'Was he okay? Like what happened?' And he said that 'Yeah, he walked out,' but there was a lot of blood."

She testified she didn't know who any of these people were, who got punched, who did the punching, or who was paying whom with what.

"Do you recall around that time having a Facebook conversation with Will in regard to Taylor Samson being missing?"

Gashus said that she did.

"I saw a link on Facebook about a missing person and I sent it to Will over Facebook and I said, 'This isn't the person that got beat up?' I was concerned about that. And he responded and said that it wasn't the same person."

Gashus agreed with the Crown that she told police when she arrived back at Will's, the apartment reeked of bleach and he told her he had poured it all over the floor to clean up.

"Will, gave you no indication at all that anyone had been shot in the apartment that night, correct?"

"No."

She told the court she had had contact with Sandeson since his arrest.

"Isn't it true that he told you that Chantale Comeau's statement to the police made him look bad?"

"Yes."

On re-direct the defence asked Gashus if she got the impression Sandeson was in any way trying to influence her testimony when he made that comment. She said she did not.

The defence lawyers looked at each other, then at Sandeson, as though they were still trying to decide whether to put him on the stand. The courtroom was silent, many desperately wanting to hear what Sandeson would have to say for himself now. Would he—could he—continue to concoct stories about Morphsuited intruders after all that evidence?

It seemed he could not.

The defence closed its case. William Sandeson did not take the stand in his own defence.

"You've heard a lot of things throughout this trial that perhaps are going to leave a poor impression with you," Eugene Tan said in his closing argument to the jury.

"What is important though is that there are going to be some things that you consider to be distasteful, perhaps his participation in the drug trade, perhaps the fact that he loaned money at what may be considered a fairly high rate to somebody. Distasteful, yes, but is that consistent with guilt?"

Tan told the jury that while they hadn't actually said the words, from the testimony of Detective Constable Roger Sayer and from the words of the Crown, they seemed to believe William Sandeson to be a criminal mastermind. Tan argued the opposite was true, that Sandeson didn't think things through. He also argued Sandeson was not in financial need, that he had a $200,000 line of credit on which there were no limitations, and so that could not be his motive for murder.

"You've got to reject that. There's just no evidence whatsoever to support that," he contended.

Tan also addressed the damning evidence provided by Justin Blades and Pookiel McCabe, pointing out Sandeson knew they were home, and, because of that, the elements of planning and deliberation required to convict a person of first-degree murder could not be present.

"Who would think to carry out this type of act in this type of apartment, knowing full well that there were people right next door?"

Tan was just getting started.

"The police, the Crown have invited you to believe that Mr. Sandeson is a cold calculated murderer who mapped out every detail and every move in advance, but look for yourself, okay. You saw exactly what happened there. You saw what happened there. Consistent with panic. Consistent with somebody who had no idea what was going to happen."

Tan acknowledged the surveillance video had become a major point in the trial, pointing out it was Sandeson himself who had installed the system.

"If Mr. Sandeson is this criminal mastermind...why on earth would he continue to let that tape roll?" Tan implored, going so far as to say if the circumstances weren't so serious, the Crown's theory would border on "ridiculous."

He pointed out Sandeson had the opportunity to get rid of his gun and other evidence after his first statement to police during which he was still a witness, but he didn't.

Tan was adamant police chose to follow the evidence that supported their theory, accusing the Crown of shoehorning the facts to fit its case.

Finally, he argued that the police investigation was inadequate, that they failed to investigate information that was before them, that they had no right to enter Sandeson's apartment when they did, that they weren't wearing protective clothing when they should have been, that they failed to take appropriate notes, and that they did a poor job of managing the evidence.

Tan claimed there was reasonable doubt on all elements of the Crown's theory, especially the element that the murder was planned and premeditated.

He asked the jury to acquit William Sandeson.

CHAPTER 16
VERDICT

On June 15, almost exactly two months after William Sandeson's murder trial began, Justice Joshua Arnold began his final instructions to the jury. He began by telling them he would explain the law and how they should use it to make a decision, not make a decision for them.

"Deciding the facts is your job, not mine," he declared.

He also explained that it wasn't up to them to answer all of the questions in this case, only to decide whether a crime was proven beyond a reasonable doubt. They were given the choice of four possible verdicts: guilty as charged of first-degree murder, guilty of second-degree murder, guilty of manslaughter, or not guilty.

Arnold told the jury they must not be influenced by fear, sympathy, or prejudice and that the verdict must be unanimous.

"Keep an open mind but not an empty head," he urged. "Don't just talk. Listen, too."

The jury began deliberating.

The city of Halifax began its countdown.

Hour after hour ticked by. Thursday turned into Friday. Then Friday turned into Saturday.

No one anticipated it would take this long.

People began to speculate. Family and friends who had been hanging around the courthouse began to worry. *What if it meant they weren't convinced beyond a reasonable doubt? What if they were going to convict him of second-degree murder instead of first?* The wait was so long people didn't know what to do with themselves. One of Taylor's friends walked into the courthouse wearing a Morphsuit. It was a search for levity that fell flat, upsetting some of the others.

Finally, on June 16, Father's Day Sunday, after three weeks of pre-trial motions, eight weeks of trial, and twenty-two hours of deliberations, the verdict was in. Taylor Samson's friends and family crowded into the courtroom, sobbing before the jury had even entered. Some had been there every day. Others had travelled from outside of Halifax to hear the moment of truth. William Sandeson's family was not present. His lawyer said Will had asked them not to be.

The jury entered the room, the foreperson stood and announced the verdict: *Guilty as charged of first-degree murder.*

There was sobbing and clapping in the courtroom. "Thank you," exclaimed one of Samson's family members.

One of the jurors was also weeping, another had tears in her eyes.

William Sandeson sat at the defence table with his lawyers, his hands clasped, showing no emotion.

For Blair Rhodes, who says he tries to be as dispassionate as possible while covering courts, providing a voice for the often-voiceless family members of victims, this case was different.

"I developed a visceral dislike for William Sandeson in this trial, the smugness that he displayed, never cracking the facade. He's the only one I've seen who showed absolutely no compassion, no empathy, nothing."

As Sandeson was brought out of the courtroom, one Samson family member shouted, "Tell us where he is!"

"Turn around and take a bow, Billy," Samson's mother yelled.

Outside, Linda Boutilier, who was in the courtroom every day, sobbed with relief, "I can actually sleep for a change. It's been hell for twenty-two months."

In Canada, a conviction of first-degree murder comes with an automatic life sentence and no chance of parole for twenty-five years. William Sandeson was formally sentenced on July 11, 2017.

Two of the jurors, whose civic duty was already complete, showed up to court anyway.

"I felt that that showed a level of engagement above and beyond what was even required or expected of them," says Rhodes.

The sentencing hearing also gave Taylor Samson's friends and family a chance to provide victim-impact statements. Eighteen of them did, although not all were presented in court.

"He was the first person outside of my family to make me feel loved," said Samson's childhood friend Ryan Wilson. "I'll never get to feel that loving friendship again. I'll never have my ribs crushed by one of his hugs again," he told the court, his voice cracking with emotion.

Kaitlynne Lowe said her own sense of security and hope had been shattered by Samson's death and that the foundation of her life had crumbled.

"It is impossible to feel safe anywhere...because I now know the horrors that can exist right next door."

"I just want to be myself again, the happy-go-lucky guy, not the one who has to wear a mask to hide his true feeling," sobbed Samson's younger brother, Connor.

Missing was a victim-impact statement from Samson's mother, Linda Boutilier.

"I wrote it probably six months after Taylor went missing," she said three weeks later. "I must have wrote about ten pages, with the tears and with the anger." She started to cry. "And I ripped it up. I thought *why bother, he doesn't care. He doesn't care of the hell that we've gone through.* If I stood there and let him see my pain, it's like

I'm empowering him. It's like he'd get enjoyment out of seeing it, and I wasn't going to do it. I refused to do it."

Justice Joshua Arnold told the court Sandeson had already spent 693 days in custody.

"In accordance with what I am mandated to do by the Criminal Code, I sentence William Sandeson to life in prison," said Arnold.

STILL NO BODY

The lawyers have since moved on, of course, both sides admitting the workload from this case was overwhelming.

"It was basically months of going to court every day, coming home, working every evening, working every weekend, without a break," says Brad Sarson in an interview after the case had concluded.

"There was more than one night where I didn't get any sleep at all and then went to court the next day," says Susan MacKay. "I'd never done that before in my career and I don't want to ever do it again."

The police still think about finding Taylor Samson's body.

"Every time that you see something on the news or you hear of somebody discovering a body or something like that, it's the first thing that comes to mind," says Detective Constable Sayer. "Constantly you're trying to piece together, you know, how could you help find the person, or could you bring them home."

It's a question that also haunts Linda Boutilier. She and her younger son have now left their home in Amherst and relocated to Halifax.

"You can't walk down the street in Amherst without people looking at you, whispering, 'That's the mother.' Or people walking up to you wanting to know—"

Connor jumps in, "'Did you hear anything yet? Is there any news yet? Did they find the body yet?'"

His mother says she got those questions too.

"'Do you think he's chopped up?' We know he's probably chopped up.'"

She still wants to know where her son is.

"I don't think there's anything to find," says Rhodes, referencing Sandeson's plan to kill his girlfriend in a fit of rage, cut off her head and hands, and dissolve her body in a bucket of lye on his parents' farm.

"That's my theory of what has become of Taylor Samson, and he sure as hell didn't deserve that."

Rhodes, trying to explain what attracts him to covering crime, says courts are a microcosm of human behaviour, showing humanity at its best and worst, both extremes under one roof.

"You look at some of these accused and they're the most miserable excuses of human beings you'd ever meet," he says. "I have been amazed at the grace of the families of victims who feel some obligation to talk as they're still coming to terms with the loss of a loved one. And you know, it means I go home at night and hug my kids a little tighter."

Boutilier desperately wants people to know her son was more than a drug dealer.

"Taylor was a kid selling marijuana to make extra money. What he did was wrong; I understand that, and a lot of people judge me, 'How can you be his mother and know that he sells marijuana?' Well guess what, honey, your kid was probably his dealer, but you just don't know it," she says.

"I am who I am. If you judge me because I'm honest, well then you're going to judge me because I'm honest."

She finds comfort in listening to YouTube tutorials her son had created to help his classmates. "I listen to it sometimes to go to sleep," she says. "I don't understand a word he's saying, it's all physics, but I still listen to it. It's his voice. It's like having him here."

According to a profile on a dating site for Canadian inmates, Sandeson is now serving his sentence in maximum security at the Donnacona Penitentiary in Quebec.

The profile reads:

CONVICTED OF: 1ˢᵗ DEGREE MURDER
EXPECTED RELEASED DATE: 2037
INTERESTED IN: CORRESPONDING WITH WOMEN

I'm currently serving 25 to life while waiting for an appeal. Formerly a medical student, I've since completed certificate programs in Paralegal and Electrical Engineering. Presently I'm finishing a MBA and looking into other correspondence education. I grew up on a farm and playing lots of sports. Phone access is pretty limited in maximum security so I'm looking to remain social through letters. I'm particularly interested in hearing from anyone working in or studying some form of healthcare but am eager to talk to people from my background. Je suis apprender Francais aussi et je voudrais escriber en Francais quand possible.

Sandeson is appealing his conviction, citing ten grounds including that his right to be secure against unreasonable search or seizure under the Canadian Charter of Rights and Freedoms was breached when police entered his apartment without a warrant, that Justice Arnold erred by not granting a mistrial, and that the jury came to an unreasonable verdict.

"I think the jury's verdict on first-degree murder is arguable," says Brad Sarson.

Author: Are you saying that you don't think the jury reached the right verdict?

Sarson: Correct.

Author: Based on the evidence?

Sarson: Based on the evidence and the law that they were instructed on.

Author to Eugene Tan: He is guilty. It's a fact that he's guilty.

Tan: Yes, it's a fact that he's guilty.

Author: Do you believe that he's guilty?

Tan: No.

Author: You don't?

Tan: No.

Author: So what is that based on? Is that based on a personal relationship with him? Is it based on that you know his family or just the evidence?

Tan: It's based on all of that. It's based on perhaps, things that I know that either would not be admissible, that we didn't bring forward, or that we didn't want to bring forward.

Author: Is there anything that you think I should know that you can tell me, that didn't come up in court?

Tan: I would love to have that conversation with you, and Will is still thinking about that, and that may be a conversation, if you have the time, if you're willing, that we may have.

It has not happened.

Sandeson has not responded to letters from the author, and his parents declined to participate in this work, saying, "This story is not over."

"I understand that they're victims too," says Taylor Samson's mother. "I can't imagine if it was around the other way."

EPILOGUE

The bizarre twists in the Sandeson case continued even after it seemed to be over. In the months following his sentencing, Will Sandeson would go on to sue the roommate with whom he was living at the time of the murder. Sandeson, it turns out, was an avid collector of shoes, specifically sneakers, and made homemade wine during his spare time. He took Dylan Zinck-Selig to small claims court in Halifax, claiming he had stolen from him after his arrest.

Court documents state Sandeson's apartment contained twenty-eight pairs of brand-name sneakers at the time police were searching it in August 2015. Many were new and most were stored in shoeboxes in his closet. According to the documents, eighteen pairs of shoes were missing when Sandeson's family went to collect them after the forensic work on the apartment was complete. Additionally, forty bottles of homemade wine and five to ten bottles of hard liquor were unaccounted for.

Sandeson believed Zinck-Selig owed him $2,500 for the items. Zinck-Selig claimed he took only two pairs of sneakers and four bottles of wine, which he felt entitled to because some of his own things were destroyed during the police search.

In the end, the adjudicator, Eric Slone, ruled Zinck-Selig was a victim of systems beyond anyone's control but did not have the right to take anything that was not his. He ordered him to pay William Sandeson $500, the value of the items he had admitted to taking, plus process-serving costs, bringing the total to $700.

If it seems William Sandeson should have had more important things to worry about it, so too did Dalhousie University.

The school has now changed its medical-school admission requirements for the first time in ten years.

Dr. Gus Grant, registrar and CEO of the College of Physicians and Surgeons of Nova Scotia, the body that regulates the province's medical profession, says the dean of the Faculty of Medicine asked him to conduct a review of the admissions process. The review committee included a member of the public as well as experts in the fields of medicine, law, diversity, university admissions, and undergraduate medical education.

Grant is quick to point out he doesn't believe the review was as a direct result of the Sandeson case, but rather to "ensure that the admissions process bolstered the Faculty of Medicine's commitment to service, excellence and broad considerations of diversity."

That said, Grant confirms his report did mention both the Stephen Tynes and Sandeson cases.

"The committee undertook this review conscious of recent cases in the public domain involving applicants accepted to Dalhousie's Medical School charged with serious crimes," the report states. "The publicity associated with these cases has cast a shadow for some on the admissions process. The question arising from the publicity is whether the admissions process takes adequate steps to screen out individuals inappropriate for a career in medicine."

"It would have been disingenuous not to mention it," Grant says in an interview. "Both those cases were very much in the public eye at the time of my generating the report....I'd heard a fair number of exasperated murmurings about *How did these people get into medical school.*"

He says Dal does a very good job in selecting students who succeed in the curriculum and succeed in practice, but the admissions
process is not an exact science.

"You're making a point-in-time assessment about a young person's ability to succeed over the course of a career in a very challenging field," he says, adding there will never be a perfect system.

"There will never be a system that will successfully weed out
psychopaths. That's one of the core abilities of the psychopath is to
avoid detection. They're more skilled at hiding their characteristics
than any trained interviewer is at identifying them."

But Grant says some of the recommendations in his report will
at least help prevent these kinds of people from getting into med
school. Acknowledging that scholarly ability is important, his committee was concerned that Dal puts too much emphasis on cogni-
tive power, placing too much weight on grade point averages and
MCAT scores.

"The day-to-day success of a doctor, the day-to-day well-being
of his or her patients is rarely dependent on the doctor's stagger-
ing genius," says Grant. "Success in medical practice is mostly
composed of compassion, consistency, empathy, diligence,
humility. Those are the more important ingredients of success
in medicine."

Dal was already screening for non-cognitive attributes, measuring extracurricular activities, volunteering, employment history, and medical experience, but the committee wasn't convinced they were good proxies to measure things like empathy
and integrity.

Further, the committee felt the means by which Dal was measuring these things was rife with inherent bias in favour of candidates from privileged backgrounds. For example, students whose
parents were physicians would be able to pay for access to tutors
and med-school preparation courses. It would also be far easier for
those candidates to accumulate an impressive exposure to medicine. The committee suggested Dal eliminate its requirement for

students to write a personal essay, which it used to look for evidence of empathy and ethical decision making, given there is no way to even prove the student actually wrote the essay.

The committee recommended Dal stop measuring extracurricular, volunteering, employment, and medical experience and begin offering candidates the opportunity to address any four of the following domains: scholar, professionalism, health advocate, collaborator, communicator, manager. It also recommended that evaluators be encouraged to "red flag" applications for discussion when concerns about a candidate arise during their interview.

After ignoring repeated requests for interviews for this book over the period of six months, Dalhousie University's senior communications manager finally responded that the school "would not be providing an interview."

ACKNOWLEDGEMENTS

In May 2017 I was sitting in courtroom 301 at Nova Scotia Supreme Court live tweeting the Sandeson trial in my role as a reporter when an email flashed across my screen. It was from Elaine McCluskey, whom I did not know, asking if I'd like to write a book about the case. I thought it might be spam.

It turned out Elaine was the real deal, and I didn't know it then, but I had just won the editor lottery! This book was her idea and she has made it so much better. Elaine, thank you for your attention to detail, for patient direction while also giving me the freedom to write this story in my own voice, and for your steadfast encouragement throughout this process. Also, thanks for choosing me.

Thank you to the entire team at Nimbus Publishing, especially Whitney Moran and Terrilee Bulger, for taking a chance on me as a first-time author.

Thank you to my employer, the CBC, and managers Nancy Waugh and Greg Reaume, who have graciously supported this project and taken the time to help ensure it respects the journalistic ethics Canadians expect.

Thank you to lawyer David Coles for the sound legal advice that provided peace of mind.

Thank you to photographers Alex and Kate MacAulay for shooting my author headshot. Your work is top notch, and I always have fun in your studio!

Thank you to Halifax Regional Police, Nova Scotia Public Prosecutions, the Nova Scotia Judiciary, and William Sandeson's defence team for seeing the value in this project and helping to facilitate it on various levels.

Thank you to my former videographer, George Reeves, who has been my constant collaborator for the better part of the last decade. I have learned so much about storytelling from you.

Thank you to my former television producer, Julie Caswell, who believed in this story, and in me, when many did not. I have always valued your news judgment. I miss chasing crime with you.

Thank you to Steve Murphy, who provided guidance for this project in more ways than I could ever begin to articulate. Your continued friendship and mentorship means so much to me.

Thank you to my partners in crime, a small but mighty bunch of Halifax reporters dedicated to covering each day of the very long Sandeson trial: Natasha Pace, then of Global TV, *Metro*'s Zane Woodford, Kieran Leavitt freelancing for *The Coast* and The Canadian Press, and my friend and colleague, the CBC's Blair Rhodes. I appreciated your collaboration...and company!

To Linda Boutilier, Dean Samson, and all of Taylor's family and friends, thank you, thank you, thank you for your participation and support and for trusting me to tell your story over and over again. Even if you are not quoted directly, know that you helped me understand the person that Taylor was. Linda gave me the first interview when Taylor went missing and I have never taken that for granted. When I told her I was considering writing a book, I also told her there would be parts of it that she might not like to read. "That's okay," she said. "I know if you write it, it will be fair." Know that I have had your voice in my head throughout this process and I have done my very best to be fair.

Finally, thank you to my own mom and dad who raised my brother, Jordan, and me in a way that gave me the courage to take on this project when it would have been much easier to say no. They have always encouraged me and never doubted me even when I quit my job to write a book! I love you.